I0096291

RETAINING YOUR
HEALTHCARE
HEROES

A HEALTHCARE LEADER'S GUIDE TO
Improving Perceptions
of **Leader Support**

JULIE KOVENCZ

Retaining Your Healthcare Heroes: A Healthcare Leader's Guide to Improving Perceptions of Leader Support © Julie Kovencz 2022

All rights reserved. No part of this publication may be reproduced, stored in retrieval system, or transmitted in any way by any means, electronic, mechanical, photocopy, recording or otherwise without the prior permission of the author except as provided by USA copyright law.

Published by Julie Kovencz

Editing: Gail Fallen
Publishing and Design Services: MelindaMartin.me
Cover Artwork: Shield by gn8/depositphotos.com
            Caduceus by Tribaliumivanka/depositphotos.com

ISBN: 979-8-9871903-0-2 (paperback)
           979-8-9871903-1-9 (epub)
           979-8-9871903-2-6 (hardback)

For my family—my support system—
who supported me through it all,
even when they didn't understand
why I was doing what I did.

Contents

A Letter to the Reader

A CAREER IN HUMAN RESOURCES WAS NOT MY INITIAL CAREER choice growing up, but when I discovered my inability to master chemistry, becoming a nuclear medicine technologist was out. However, I knew I wanted to do something in the healthcare field, and I wanted to do something that would allow me to help people. So I went the business route midway through earning my bachelor's degree and discovered my love for human resources and being able to help people in another way.

Being in human resources, you need to be a people person. Not only are you usually the first department a new employee interacts with but also usually the last. One of the most important things I have learned throughout my career is sometimes people need someone to listen to them, to hear them. Whether it be a leader needing direction on how to handle a situation or an employee voicing a concern, they want someone to hear them and talk things through with them. And as simple as that sounds, it does not happen enough in most organizations. Do not get me wrong; it isn't always an easy thing and does not solve all the issues, but giving someone your attention and time can help significantly.

Sometimes, as leaders, it is hard for us to slow down and listen to the needs of our employees. Usually, we deal with several issues at once and have other pressures to contend with, like meeting both productivity and financial goals, let alone staff concerns. This guide is essential to me because I think that leaders sometimes focus on the sizable issues and miss opportunities to identify employee concerns before they escalate into significant ones. Additionally, I feel it is beneficial for leaders to develop relationships with their employees, take the extra time to talk to them, and understand what they deal with on a daily basis. It always amazes me when I have leaders that do not want to address issues or concerns with employees and vice versa.

I have started most chapters with either a story or questions for you to consider while reading the material. Then, at the end of each chapter, I have included a summary of the ideas presented and some reflection questions for consideration. I hope this guide will help you reflect on your current leadership style and find solutions to help retain employees within your organization.

CHAPTER 1

Introduction and Personal Story

*A good objective of leadership is
to help those who are doing poorly to do well
and to help those who are doing well to do even better.*

—JIM ROHN

HEALTHCARE LEADERS FACE A VAST ARRAY OF CHALLENGES. Healthcare has faced staff shortages over many years, and the global pandemic has intensified the shortage. According to *U.S. News & World Report*, about 20 percent of healthcare workers have quit since the COVID-19 pandemic,[1] increasing the stress on an already strained industry. In addition, shortages have caused compensation to become increasingly competitive, leaving some facilities unable to match the pay at larger organizations. Overall, healthcare leaders face staffing shortages, a lack of candidates to fill open positions, and budget restrictions. The shortages have led to an increased need for employee retention because there are no people waiting to fill empty positions, so leaders must retain the employees they have now. Leaders have also seen a change in the workforce they employ, like generational differences, which they are also trying to navigate. So what can leaders do to retain their current staff?

Fortunately, leaders can do little things to help employees feel supported without spending excessive money or magically finding staff. But, unfortunately, sometimes leaders focus so much on the things they cannot do because of the cost or unrealistic expectations that the easy things they can do slip right past them, like providing better employee support.

Working in human resources allows me to see situations from both an employee's *and* a leader's view. Over my fourteen years of being in human resources, a common theme that has continued to emerge is the need for employees to feel supported by their leader. Conversely, I have often seen leaders lose good employees over some of the simplest things.

For example, I have spoken with team members who tell their leaders that they are stretched too thin and need help, which falls on deaf ears. Or, in other instances, some leaders are so disconnected that they don't know their team members' daily challenges, and they don't even ask! In addition, I have seen organizations offer employees more money to retain them, and they still leave because they are unhappy. These challenges leave frustrated leaders and team members struggling to meet the organization's needs.

This need for support happens at all levels, whether an employee needs support from their team leader or a director needs support from their administrator. Regardless of the level, the need for support is still there. The need for leaders, at any level, to understand how they make their employees feel is critical. The way an employee is left feeling about their job determines whether they will be back the next day, and leaders affect that feeling more than they know.

Support can mean many things, and its definition changes based on a person's needs and perceptions. There are times when a leader may be doing everything possible to support their team members, but some may feel it is not enough, or they do not see or know what their leaders are doing. Supportive leadership involves building trust, providing encouragement, communicating, and helping team members overcome the challenges they face.[2]

Unfortunately, when team members become overwhelmed at work, they look to their leaders to fix things quickly. In healthcare, we often face staffing shortages, leading to challenges that leaders cannot quickly fix, which leads to staff feeling like their leaders are not doing enough to help. In addition, studies show that lower levels of perceived organizational support increase cynicism across the organization.[3]

I entered human resources because I care about people, and I have always enjoyed being able to help others. Over the last fourteen years, my career has mainly been in the healthcare industry, and though healthcare is like other service industries, it is also unique. I know that so many different situations happen in the workplace, and we cannot always make everyone happy. I also understand that we face an entirely different generational workforce, which adds new challenges for leaders. Additionally, I have leaders who do everything to support their staff, and their staff still leave or feel there is no support. We also face staff burnout and stiff competition within healthcare. However, I feel there are times when leaders need to take a step back and evaluate a situation before just acting on it. Leaders can balance organizational needs and employee satisfaction by knowing and understanding what their employees want, leading to happier employees and satisfied leaders.

The relationships between leaders and team members are critical to any organization. Relationship building and doing what is suitable for employees positively affect organizations, yet many leaders fall short in these areas. If the work relationships between leaders and team members are effective, both parties will benefit.[4] Leaders will have different relationships with their team members; however, they must understand the types of relationships their team members want.

For example, some team members look to have a high-quality relationship with their leader. They are interested in taking on additional responsibilities, having growth opportunities, and becoming more team oriented. Then you have other team members who care nothing about growing further within the organization; they come to work to do their job and are perfectly happy with their position within the team. These lower-quality relationships are also critical to the organization, and leaders need to focus on both groups and develop their relationships as needed.

Is there one answer that will solve everyone's issues? Of course not. But are there things leaders can do to retain their current team members? One hundred percent, *yes*.

This guide will first outline some of the current challenges that healthcare leaders face today, followed by what employees want and expect from their leaders. Next, this guide will show how positive leader support can affect job satisfaction, how leader trust can impact employee retention, and how leader communication can affect current staff. These different areas of leader impact can ultimately determine the types of relationships between leaders and their employees and eventually determine staff turnover intentions. Finally, this guide will examine different strategies that leaders can take to improve the feelings of leader support, leader trust, and leadership communication. I will also discuss strategies to improve the relationships between leaders and employees and the overall organizational implications of improved leader support.

While reading this guide, I hope that you will be able to identify with specific examples given and ultimately find ways you can support your employees more effectively. I have also included some reflection questions at the end of several chapters to help you reflect more on the chapter's content and connect it to your organization.

CHAPTER 1

Introduction and Personal Story

Key Points

- ❖ All employees need to feel supported, no matter their level.

- ❖ Support comes in many different forms and means different things to different people.

- ❖ Relationships are critical between a leader and an employee within an organization.

Current Challenges

Our ability to handle life's challenges
is a measure of our strength of character.

—LES BROWN

How often in your career have you heard employees say—or have even said yourself—"I am overworked. I don't want to be here anymore. I hate my job but love my coworkers. Why are there never enough people working? They pay five dollars more an hour down the street. This company does not appreciate our hard work. Where did all the fun things go that the company used to offer? Where is my leader when I need them? I work too hard for what I get paid. I can leave here and go somewhere that appreciates me"? And the list could probably go on and on.

As mentioned in chapter 1, healthcare leaders face many challenges with employees. These challenges include but are certainly not limited to staffing shortages, a lack of candidates to fill open positions, staff burnout, onboarding and retaining new employees, lack of communication, and increasingly competitive compensation between healthcare facilities. Burnout and job dissatisfaction result in healthcare workers taking early retirements, moving to higher-paid traveling positions, switching careers, or exiting the healthcare industry entirely.[1] Additionally, data show that 56 percent of registered nurses leave the healthcare field to find less stressful work.[2]

Unfortunately, all these challenges relate to one another.

For example, a lack of applicants to fill open positions leads to staffing shortages, which leads to employee burnout.

All these challenges have significantly impacted turnover and retention. As a result, retaining staff has become a top priority throughout the healthcare industry. Job satisfaction is an essential factor in maintaining an experienced and skilled workforce. Leaders should understand that job satisfaction leads to higher productivity, increased communication, and better cooperation with team members, ultimately resulting in fewer people looking to leave.

A Lack of Candidates

Positions that previously had numerous applicants now see few to none, which leaves leaders scrambling when they lose employees. Across all industries, job seekers are more selective and expect something different from organizations than ever before.[3] According to an article on Indeed.com, job seekers' interest in healthcare has declined. In addition, the COVID-19 pandemic caused people to leave the healthcare industry altogether. As a result, the number of unemployed healthcare workers is the lowest it has ever been, resulting in a tight healthcare labor market and a significant labor supply/demand disparity.[4] Limited skilled and experienced employees can backfill those positions as people leave healthcare. Unfortunately, I have also seen these shortages guide leaders to hiring less than stellar employees. I have specifically asked leaders, "Would you have hired this person two years ago?" and I am continually told, "No."

Unfortunately, there is not the same caliber of applicants as there once was, and leaders need to adapt. In addition, as the US population ages and the world settles into the new normal after a global pandemic, the demand for healthcare services will rise, resulting in the healthcare industry continuing to need more employees.[5] Between losing experienced workers and a limited number of applicants, leaders have to become more creative with staffing, but they also need to be more aware of their staff's needs.

Healthcare Staff Shortages

Healthcare facilities face staff shortages, and this challenge does not seem to be abating. The US Bureau of Labor Statistics anticipates that healthcare employment will grow 16 percent from 2020 to 2030, increasing the demand for healthcare workers.[6] However, healthcare job openings are at historic highs and are the highest in any industry,[7] resulting in organizations feeling the pressure of not having enough staff.

The World Health Organization projects a worldwide shortage of eighteen million healthcare workers by 2030.[8] These staggering numbers lead facilities to partner with local schools to recruit graduates of healthcare programs. Fortunately, according to the American Association of Colleges of Nursing, there has been a significant increase in the enrollment numbers for nursing programs; however, in 2020, over eighty thousand candidates were denied entry into programs due to a shortage of clinical sites and faculty and resources.[9] Unfortunately, with the demand for healthcare professionals continually increasing, the growing gap between supply and demand from healthcare programs can't meet the demand.

Staffing shortages do not change the industry's demand, and leaders still expect their employees to provide the same quality work whether they have an entire staff or not. As a result, organizational leaders expect employees to do more work with fewer resources. Working with less staff affects certain aspects like quality of care, patient satisfaction, poorer patient outcomes, and employee burnout, resulting in leaders facing severe challenges when satisfying employees, patients, organizational, and regulatory expectations. In addition, I have seen leaders' expectations of staff waver and staff accountability decrease due to leaders being fearful of staff leaving and having another opening.

Onboarding & Retaining New Employees

The experiences that new employees have when they begin at a new organization are critical to whether they will stay. Studies show that approximately 20 percent of new employees leave within forty-five days of starting their new position.[10] Whether an employee decides the position is not a fit for them, or the leader decides the employee is not a fit for the organization, the leader is left with another vacancy. In addition, when new employees start at an organization, they look for a welcoming environment and expect to be treated as if the organization is happy to have them. Unfortunately, I have seen new employees sent to their department after orientation, and staff won't even show them around the department, let alone be welcoming.

Onboarding a new employee is the organization's opportunity to make an excellent first impression and help show the new employee they made the right choice in choosing the organization. However, leaders must understand that they need to engage and encourage new employees, which will help retain the employee.[11] New employees have less onboarding and training time due to the staffing issues and shortages that healthcare facilities face. Therefore, expectations are that they pick up quickly, leading to new employees looking to leave. Leaders must understand that even though they are short-staffed, new employees need to have meaningful onboarding and training time, and it is up to the leader to ensure that new employees have received the proper training they need.

Lack of Communication

The topic of communication seems to always come up during staff surveys and exit interviews as something employees feel is lacking. Unfortunately, this topic is a challenge that all leaders and organizations face. Leaders need to maintain an open line of communication so that employees are aware of changes within the organization. It is also critical for leaders to let employees know that they hear and are aware of their concerns. Within organizations, approachable and involved leaders create a climate of open communication that monitors the culture within their departments.[12] By providing an environment with open communication, leaders invite employees to discuss concerns, allowing leaders to inform employees what they are doing to address those concerns.

For example, leaders need to be up front with employees about what they are doing to help hire new staff or what challenges they may be having with hiring. At least this way, employees know that their leaders are attempting to help with the staffing shortages.

In his book, Levi also discussed how communication is essential to a team and that good communication skills can affect the organizational climate and culture.[13] Without good communication, leaders lose a critical aspect of feeling connected with their teams.

The Feeling of Burnout

Working understaffed ultimately leads to employees being exhausted mentally and physically . . . and ultimately burned out. In addition, staffing shortages, increased responsibilities, and governmental regulations also contribute to burnout among healthcare staff.[14] As a result, not only does burnout cause employees to leave their healthcare jobs but it also is causing people to leave the healthcare industry altogether, which leads to organizations spending more money on recruiting, training, and retaining employees.[15]

In addition, burnout affects job performance, patient safety, personal demeanor, relationships, and overall quality of life.[16] Burnout is not an exclusive problem. As research shows, it affects much more than just the employee, resulting in organizations needing to be aware of how burnout affects their employees and patients. Burnout also affects team relationships and job satisfaction and can lead to strained relationships in an already stressful environment.[17] But burnout does not just affect employees at a staff level; it also affects leaders at all levels.

Regardless of the management level, there has been a significantly growing problem with leader burnout, which was particularly evident in 2021.[18] Research shows that 66 percent of leaders said they had suffered from burnout over that year.[19] Unfortunately, leaders have been responsible for managing their employees' challenges. Employees look to them to bring in additional staff or schedule more staff to help in needed areas, and leaders cannot meet those expectations. I have also had leaders tell me that the expectation is to maintain productivity levels with the known shortages. Recent studies show that 72 percent of leaders feel increased pressure to deliver results, while 84 percent feel responsible for the burnout of their employees.[20] The reality is that front-line leaders try to comfort their employees and retain them while not having the answers themselves and feeling overwhelmed.

Unfortunately, the burnout among leaders is just getting worse.[21] Burnout among leaders and employees is critical, leading to even more resignations and shortages.

Healthcare Competition

When employees face burnout and dissatisfaction, they look for another job, leading to more shortages. Unfortunately, the number of open jobs far outnumbers the workforce, resulting in employees making rash decisions to leave. Additionally, compensation is a critical component that employees consider when deciding whether to stay in their current job.[22] Unfortunately, right now, the competition between healthcare entities is exorbitant. Lately, candidates come to interview and have a few offers they can choose from, so it is a game of who can offer the candidates the most.

Healthcare facilities have increased their recruiting techniques and strive to make their facilities more attractive to those looking to change. Due to staffing shortages across the healthcare industry, healthcare workers can pretty much choose where they want to go. Unfortunately for leaders, if an employee becomes dissatisfied with something in their current role, they can leave and find another position at another healthcare facility within days (if not hours).

Increased open positions have led to increased competition between healthcare facilities, resulting in increased wages offered for most positions. The shortage of healthcare workers has hampered recruitment and retention and driven up wages.[23] Unfortunately, smaller facilities cannot compete with more extensive facilities with more financial resources. Some larger facilities are not only offering higher hourly rates but also large sign-on bonuses. Yet those higher wages do not lead to increased satisfaction. Due to dissatisfaction, I have seen people leave their jobs for more money, only to return within ninety days. Money is not always the solution, nor is it the only solution when employees feel the stress of staff shortages and burnout.

With all these challenges, I feel leaders face some of the biggest ones: determining how to keep employees feeling satisfied, meeting the organization's needs, and facing the challenges above. In addition, they have the challenging task of balancing all the above while still being successful leaders in an organization. I feel that leaders, especially with the challenges they face today, may struggle to keep employees satisfied and hold them accountable to productivity standards.

Unfortunately, employees know healthcare facilities face challenges, and some take advantage of the staffing strains.

I have seen employees call off to be spiteful for not getting their way, and, unfortunately, it leaves the leader with their hands tied. In contrast, some employees get upset because they feel leaders are not holding people accountable to the rules or are being consistent with policies. So, again, it is a balancing act that leaders need to figure out, and ultimately it comes down to truly understanding what employees need to satisfy their job needs.

CHAPTER 2
Current Challenges

Key Points

❖ Organizations face several different challenges.

❖ Leaders need to focus on the challenges they can make the most impact on, like communication and retention.

Reflection Questions

❖ What are some current struggles that you are seeing within your organization?

❖ Do you see that struggles throughout the organization are more concentrated in certain areas?

CHAPTER 3

What Do Employees Want?

Employees who believe that management is concerned about them as a whole person—not just an employee—are more productive, more satisfied, more fulfilled. Satisfied employees mean satisfied customers, which leads to profitability.

—ANNE M. MULCAHY

To begin the next chapter, think about these questions: Have you ever sat down and listed out what characteristics make up your ideal job/organization? Are there specific qualities that you look for from your leader and organization? Are your ideals realistic? If you find yourself not getting what you want, do you look elsewhere? Are there needs you are willing to be flexible with or negotiate?

WHAT DO EMPLOYEES WANT? WITH THE CHALLENGES LEADERS face today, this topic is a million-dollar question. The research found that more than 90 percent of employees consider changing their jobs![1] Therefore, organizations must understand the factors that positively or negatively influence intentions to quit and what their employees want.[2] If money were the only answer, the facilities offering high incentives would not be facing the same staffing challenges as the smaller ones. However, money is not necessarily retaining employees; instead, it acts as a band-aid. I think that, initially, people believe that money will make them happier in their positions; however, money will not help their feelings of burnout or being overwhelmed. Paying an employee more will not fill those empty slots on the schedule. So a much deeper solution is needed. Of course, all employees like a pay increase, but organizations need to look at more than just increasing pay to retain their current staff. Achieving a close connection between employee preferences and organizational needs provides a business with a distinct competitive advantage by attracting and retaining talented and motivated employees.[3] The different ways that leaders can help support their employees is something that organizations need to focus on, and understanding what employees want is critical. The essential things employees want, discussed below, are leader support, promotions, flexibility, and empathy.

Leader Support

I have discussed leader support in previous chapters, and it is one of the most critical things that employees look for from their leaders. Leader support can mean different things, and it can encompass a lot. When employees look for support, they look to their leaders to understand and hear their concerns. Employees want leaders who they perceive as understanding the daily challenges they face. Employees also want recognition and appreciation for their hard work and loyalty through the challenges.[4] Finally, employees want to know that their leaders recognize what they are dealing with and work alongside them if possible. I have had employees tell me that they wish their leaders would take the time to work alongside them and see what they are dealing with instead of just coming to the department to address staff when something is wrong.

Research shows that employees who do not feel supported by their leaders experience ten times more job stress than those who feel supported.[5] Furthermore, organizations must support the leaders who support the employees, affecting job satisfaction and ultimately affecting retention.[6] Leaders who support their employees give them a sense of comfort and belonging. And employees tend to stay where they feel they belong.[7] Employees with a sense of belonging look to stay with their organization by seeking promotions to advance and grow. If employees feel their leaders support them, they are also more likely to have a deeper trust and better communication with an overall better relationship between leader and employee.

Promotions

The feeling of appreciation comes with the desire for promotions and salary increases. Organizations can show their appreciation and support of the time and talent of their employees by promoting them into higher positions of responsibility and paying them more money.[8] One survey found that 47 percent of people look for promotions for the money. The same survey found that 24 percent of people look for promotions due to the greater responsibility of a higher position.[9]

By promoting employees, organizations are empowering leadership among their employees. Through empowering leadership, organizations enhance employees' sense of control, deepen their knowledge of the organization, and increase their investment, stimulating their sense of ownership.[10] Employees with a higher sense of ownership will stay with an organization and continue to help the organization be successful.

There are different views on whether an organization should promote or hire externally for leadership positions. I think it all depends on the needs of the organization. If the organization has qualified staff to move into a role, they should do it. Employees at organizations that hire and promote within stay 41 percent longer than employees at organizations with lower internal promotion rates.[11] However, an organization should not just promote within because it is easier or to appease the current staff. An organization could do itself a disservice if it promotes someone not fully qualified for the role, ultimately leading to dissatisfied staff. Employees want to grow in organizations where they feel comfortable and believe in the overall vision. More than half of the respondents from the research survey stated that factors other than money were the best part of being promoted.[12] Ultimately, it is up to the organization's leaders to identify their top performers and place them in positions that will benefit both the employee and the organization.

Flexibility & Empathy

Out of the pandemic grew the demand for flexibility.[13] Unfortunately, most clinical positions cannot offer flexibility regarding the working location in healthcare. However, flexibility can also mean offering a flexible schedule or hours so that the front-line workers can schedule around their needs at home. Additionally, for those positions that can be remotely located, like scheduling, business office operations, etc., organizations can offer remote options to employees, which can help retain more talent. Around 65 percent of employees say flexible scheduling and remote work options will improve their work experience and loyalty.[14] Another advantage for organizations that can offer remote work is the candidate pool opens up because they can now employ candidates in different locations.[15] As the healthcare environment changes and the demands of job seekers change, it will be imperative for healthcare organizations to look at their positions and determine different ways they can offer employees more flexibility in *their* positions.

Organizations that offer more flexibility understand the importance of adapting to their employees' needs and show they support those needs. By doing this, leaders are more empathetic by attempting to put themselves in their employees' shoes. Leaders must have successful conversations with their teams by being able to feel or experience empathy and craft empathic responses when employees bring leaders their concerns.[16] Leaders who show more empathy toward their employees listen carefully to their team and their feelings while also understanding how they receive those communications.[17] An empathic communication style helps leaders explore deeply into the views and needs of their employees and achieve a better understanding of the specific concerns that need more attention.[18]

For leaders to retain their current employees, it is critical for leaders to be authentic and show their employees that they care while also engaging with their employees and keeping their teams connected.[19] Empathy is an essential trait for leaders because it helps employees feel as though they are essential and that the organization and their leader care about their well-being. These feelings help give employees a sense of belonging and a desire to stay.

The list of employee wants could go on and on. However, I identified these three areas because I feel that they are ones that leaders can adequately address and be aware of while having significant impacts on their employees. All are equally critical to employee satisfaction, and ultimately all connect under leader support, which will be the main focus of this guide.

The following chapters will further dissect leadership support, specifically leader trust and communication. Leader trust and communication are crucial elements of leader support and significantly impact the relationships between leaders and employees. The following chapters will also identify specific strategies and implications for improving employee feelings of leader support, trust, and communication. We will also examine strategies to improve leader and employee relationships along with organizational implications of improved leader support.

 CHAPTER 3

What Do Employees Want?

Key Points

❖ Employees want different things; the goal is to identify their needs.

❖ Identify the top performers within your team and understand their goals within the organization.

❖ Be flexible where you can.

Reflection Questions

❖ What do you think your employees want?

❖ Do you think your employees want a deeper connection with you as their leader?

❖ What do you think your employees want from your organization that they are not getting now?

Leader Support

Great leaders are supportive. They encourage, care, and support their teams when in need. They have the ability and willingness to sacrifice their self-interest for a greater purpose.

—ANEES HAIDARY

I came to work this morning feeling more upbeat and told myself it would be a good day! However, it is Wednesday morning, and the mood on the floor seems to be down again. When I look at the board in the nurse's station, I see that we have some high-acuity patients, and we have had some staff call in, leaving us short-staffed yet again. My charge nurse is setting patient assignments, and we all have full patient loads. The floor is bustling, and we all are barely keeping up with the things we need to do to keep our patients safe and happy.

As I walk into a patient's room, I see our manager, Lauren, walk into her office without even stopping by the nurse's station to see how things are looking. I think to myself, *Another day where we bust our butts, and she doesn't even care.* My coworkers and I never see Lauren walk through the department throughout the day. Several people who have patients in rooms near her office noticed that she was in there all day chatting with other managers or doing things on her cell phone. I hear mumbles around the nurse's station like *Why doesn't she come out here and help us? Or even check to see if we need anything, like a bathroom break or lunch?*

This behavior is an everyday occurrence for us, so none of us are surprised when we see her leave at five without as much as a wave goodbye. The lack of support that we get is frustrating and why we constantly lose staff. By the end of the day, we are exhausted and frustrated. But I love my patients, so I continue, hoping someday soon, someone will see that we need some support.

Healthcare leaders hear many complaints from their staff about being short-staffed, burned out, dissatisfied with perceived leadership support, and unhappy with the organization. Leaders hear these complaints from their staff daily and are running out of ways to answer these concerns. However, despite the challenges facing healthcare today, a leader's support and understanding can enforce employees' positive perception of leadership behaviors. In return, employees will devote more resources to their work and feel more satisfied.[1]

When employees feel supported by their leader, it positively affects their job satisfaction. Job satisfaction is a positive emotional state about one's job experience.[2] Unfortunately, the increase in exhaustion and burnout has impacted employees' expectations for their job. The more an employee's expectations overlap with the actual returns from their job, the higher their job satisfaction will be.[3] Job satisfaction is essential in maintaining an experienced and skilled workforce and leads to higher productivity, increased communication, and better cooperation with coworkers and leaders.[4] During tough times and staffing shortages, employee expectations significantly impact whether they stay with an organization.

Healthcare leaders must understand that employees need to feel supported to retain them. Leaders must understand what employees feel constitutes leader support to understand employee expectations. Leaders who support their staff show that the organization encourages and supports staff development.[5] Not only does leader support help with the retention of staff but it also improves production and overall morale. We need to define and expand on the actual context of leader support and what it entails.

Next, I discuss simple things that leaders can do daily to show their employees support. Finally, we'll look at how leader support ties to organizational support and how critical both are to employee needs.

Leader Support

I feel that leader support can be defined and perceived in many ways. One definition of leader support is valuing the employees and making them feel valued.[6] In addition, leader support involves building trust and inspiration and helping employees overcome the challenges they encounter every day.[7] Leaders who support their employees add value by encouraging teamwork and improving organizational commitment and job satisfaction by paying attention to employees' relationships and needs.[8]

For example, a leader who understands the unique relationships among their employees and identifies individual needs adds value to an employee's job experience.

Support of a leader or the positive relationship between leaders and employees is a job resource that positively affects effective job performance.[9] We have seen that the more employees feel they are supported by their leader, the more productive and satisfied that team seems to be. And a leader's support for employees in terms of resources is more likely to facilitate employees' acknowledgment of leadership behaviors and improvement of their perception of leader support.[10]

As we have discussed, leaders can show they support their employees in many different ways. It does not always have to be through promotions or salary increases. The leaders who can show they support their employees by using all their resources as leaders are the ones who can retain their employees better.

How to Show Support

Simple things that leaders can do daily to show their support for their staff include acknowledging their employees' concerns and struggles, involving higher levels of leadership when situations arise that need it, choosing incentives wisely when needing staff to put in extra time, encouraging and allowing work-life balance, and providing employees with needed resources for self-care.[11]

For example, I remember having an employee come to me very upset because they had gone to their manager to speak with them about some concerns. The entire time the employee talked, the manager was texting and did not even look up at the employee even once. Finally, the employee became so frustrated that they just walked away.

This instance is a prime example of a manager not showing their support or acknowledging their employee's concerns. Of course, everyone is busy, but one of the simplest things a leader can do is take the time to show their employees that they care enough to listen to them actively.

Involving higher levels of leadership when situations arise that merit their input is another simple thing that leaders can do to show they support their employees. In my experience, the front-line managers are dealing with several different situations at once and must determine those that require more attention by upper leadership. Of course, I understand that leaders do not want to involve their bosses unless they need to. Still, I have seen several instances where leaders try to handle situations alone, leaving employees feeling that the leader is not addressing their concerns.

For example, I had an instance where I received a call from an employee who had an ongoing issue with a coworker for several months. The employee had emails where they had contacted their leader with no response, and, after several months, the situation had escalated to where there was a physical altercation.

When I reached out to the leader, they had felt they addressed it as best they could but said they did not know what to do. Thankfully, the employee had reached out to me, and we were able to address the concerns and retain the employee in a different part of the organization.

It is always tricky when an employee brings their concerns forward, especially when it involves coworkers, as you cannot tell them how you will address the situation. However, you can respond and let the employee know that you will look into and address their concerns, not just ignore them.

Healthcare is an industry that is a 24/7 operation in most cases. So, yes, you have clinics and physician offices, but for the most part, healthcare needs are more than just 8 to 5, Monday through Friday.

Due to the staffing shortages and higher numbers of critical patients seen, healthcare employees are experiencing greater levels of burnout. As mentioned in a previous chapter, burnout has increased at all levels of healthcare. When leaders need to fill empty slots in the schedule, they need to incentivize their employees wisely—for example, looking to switch days off to cover holes in the schedule. So instead of taking away a day off from an employee, they just change it to a different day. Leaders need to be aware that employees will help, but they still need to maintain a work-life balance. Yes, employees will pick up an extra shift for the overtime. Still, leaders cannot expect their employees to work nonstop without consequences, whether those consequences are a safety issue that happens or employees getting so burned out that they quit. This situation is where leaders need to be aware of the needs of both their employees and the organization and do what they can to ensure their employees are having their needs met while ensuring the organization is still flourishing.

Then the question arises about how leaders can make their employees happy while ensuring the organization continues forward while being short-staffed. And that's where leaders look for creative solutions and also organizational support.

Organizational Support

Perceived organizational support is a perception by employees concerning the level of interest they feel the organization has in the welfare of employees and whether the organizational values meet the employee expectations.[12] Perceived organizational support leads to positive outcomes for employees, such as performance, commitment, and positive feelings.[13] Employees may feel support from their leaders, and they may see that their leaders try to help them but have their hands tied by the organization or higher leadership.

Conversely, employees can perceive a lack of organizational support. Sometimes there is such a disconnect between employees, front-line leaders, and upper management that employees can see that the organization does not support making changes no matter what their leader does.

For example, front-line leaders are making staffing situations work to the best of their ability. Still, when the organization wants to open another service line that requires more staff, they expect their front-line managers to make it work, regardless of how they do it.

The organization does not see that its leaders must beg and incentivize people to cover shifts while maintaining productivity as though there were no staffing issues. Situations like these drive leaders to burn out and even leave their leadership roles.

Instead, organizations can show support to both their leaders and employees by getting the front-line staff involved in the planning and creation of action plans.[14] Upper leadership can get buy-in from their front-line staff before making decisions that may cause more stress on an already stressful situation. Also, by including other layers of employees and leadership, upper management can check in on their employees to look for signs of stress and burnout. I think that the organizations that can identify and react proactively to the strains of their staff are more likely to retain their employees than those organizations that only react when something happens.

As discussed, leader support relies heavily on their employees' perceptions. Therefore, whether a leader feels they are being supportive or not, if their employees perceive that they do not have support, it will affect their job satisfaction and productivity. I always tell people that perception is reality, whether right or wrong, which means that the responsibility falls on leaders to identify the specific needs of their employees while showing support in many different ways.

Remember that leader support can encompass many different things and cover several employee areas. In addition, several variables can impact the perceptions of leader support. The three areas I will focus on in the following chapters are leader trust, leader communication, and leader-employee relationships.

 CHAPTER 4

Leader Support

Key Points

❖ Support is essential for the retention of employees.

❖ Show employees you care by acknowledging their concerns.

❖ Support is the responsibility of the whole organization, not just front-line leaders.

Reflection Questions

❖ Do you check in with your staff daily?

❖ When things seem overwhelming in your department, do you jump in to help?

❖ Does your organization schedule time when there are no meetings so that leaders can do the things needed within their departments?

Leader Trust

Your words and deeds must match
if you expect employees to trust in your leadership

—KEVIN KRUSE

I love my night shift team. So many of us have worked together for many years, and we have developed a robust and dependable team.

As the charge nurse on nights, my shift starts a little earlier than my team's so that I can come in, get a report from the day charge, and touch base with our manager, Brandon. Although Brandon has been in his role for a few years now, I don't deal with him much as he is usually on his way out not long after I start. However, when I take issues to him, he tends to put them back on me to resolve.

For example, lately, with the hiring of new staff, there are some things like room stocking that aren't happening during the day, so when the night shift comes in, rooms are missing vital resources. I now have my team check their rooms when they first get here so that we aren't in the middle of patient care and missing a critical item.

I took this concern to Brandon several weeks ago, and we still have the issue. I finally brought it up to the day charge nurse during our morning report. She told me that Brandon had told her about it previously, but he told her that I was complaining that the day shift wasn't doing their job. He didn't tell her about the incident that night and why it was such a big deal, nor did he seem to understand himself. He also proceeded to tell her that the night shift didn't understand how busy things were during the day and didn't want to have to stock rooms when we came in at night.

So I told her what *really* happened. We had a patient who wasn't responding, and when the nurse went to get the code started, she was missing some necessary items. This delay in resources caused a significant patient care delay, and we almost lost the patient. The day charge nurse had no idea this happened, and when we looked further into it, there had been a new staff member in that room who hadn't restocked the room. She promised to follow up with her team to ensure they trained the new staff appropriately and did what they needed before leaving their shift.

I'm still not sure why Brandon didn't handle the situation better or even care to investigate further. Instead of thinking I was complaining, he could have addressed it with the day shift. I don't trust that he will take care of issues that I bring to him and instead will speak poorly of me to my peers.

What does it mean to have leader trust, and what impact does trust have on employee retention? A large part of feeling supported includes an employee being able to have trust in their leader.

Quality relationships between leaders and their employees have a high degree of trust. However, trust in a leader and employee relationship goes both ways. Employees want to know that they can trust their leaders to be there in times of need. When employees trust their leaders, they expect to receive valuable support and have a high-quality relationship, leading to positive outcomes.[1] As a leader, I have had to prove to my employees that they can trust me by showing them that I am there to back them up, not steering them in the wrong direction and not throwing them under the bus, in addition to showing them that I am a resource for them. If I don't know an answer, I will find it with them.

Trust focuses on employees' perceptions of the leader's character, such as competency, integrity, care, and concern for others, affecting employee morale which is critical to understanding leader effectiveness and employee attitudes and behaviors.[2] In return, leaders trust that their employees will show up when scheduled and perform their job with no issues. As an employee, I trust that my leader will be forthcoming with information that will make me successful in my position and that they'll be there for support if I need them to be.

This chapter will define trust and explain how trust affects employee satisfaction and intention to stay while also looking at the positive implications of a high-trust relationship and the negative implications of a low-trust relationship.

The Perception of Trust

When we are young, trust is telling our best friend a secret. However, as we get older, we realize there is much more involved. Whether it be whom we trust to keep us safe, confide in, or support us when we need help, trust goes deeper than just secrets. So what about trust in a work environment?

Trust is "the willingness of a party to be vulnerable to the actions of another party based on the expectation that the other will perform a particular action important to the trustor."[3] In other words, trust is the degree of confidence that someone has in another's competence and belief they will always act in a fair, ethical, and predictable manner.[4]

For example, when someone accepts a position at a healthcare organization, that person trusts that the organization acts ethically and provides quality patient care.

Trust is different at every level of an organization.

For example, employees may trust their team members and not their leader. Or they may trust their leader but not their organization's administration. In addition, depending on the experiences, interactions, and context within which the relationship exists, trust can be strengthened or weakened.[5]

For example, employees expect their leaders to ensure that they have the resources they need to complete their jobs while also ensuring that employees have whatever critical things they need. Finally, leaders provide the team with organizational components that simplify the path for employees to reach the organization's corresponding goal.[6] If leaders provide their employees with the resources they need, they will reach their goals.

Employees expect their organization to keep them safe and pay them for their work. However, when the pandemic started and healthcare organizations, among many others, implemented precautions like stopping elective surgeries and wellness visits, employees in some areas were furloughed or let go for lack of work. These actions caused distrust within organizations because employees felt the organization did not support them and just let them go, and employees no longer felt safe.

We see that trust affects how employees feel toward their job and their desire to stay at an organization. Research shows the positive and negative implications when an employee trusts their leader and organization and what happens when that trust is missing. Therefore, leaders need to understand both the good and bad things that trust may affect.

Positive Implications

When there is leader trust, an employee's willingness to be vulnerable depends on the positive expectations of a leader's actions.[7] Therefore, employees who trust their key leaders are likely to exhibit positive attitudes and behaviors.[8]

Research has shown positive effects of leader trust in other areas: increased communication, cooperation, knowledge sharing, performance, stability, and overall satisfaction. When employees have a high level of trust in their leaders' fairness and ethics, they are more willing to share their expertise and skill with other team members to further their own and the organization's interests.[9] Leaders will use these employees to train new staff because they are willing to share their knowledge of the job/organization with new team members coming on board. In addition, these employees are whom a leader will go to when there's a new policy or procedure that the leader will need to implement. These employees will usually help support the leader with whatever change is coming and help get others on board.

A high level of trust increases communication between employees and leaders. Conversely, employees who do not trust, do not share information, are not open for discussion, and are less effective at problem-solving.[10] When leaders communicate and share information with employees, employees are likely to respond by communicating more often and openly with leaders on various topics.[11]

For example, when employees and leaders communicate openly, employees are more likely to share their concerns with the leaders and give their input on fixing things that may be lacking. If employees don't think their leader cares or takes their input seriously, they will not say anything. Employees are on the front lines; their input can be invaluable to leaders, so keeping it to themselves could be detrimental to an organization. Communication from front-line employees will assist leaders in understanding what is working—and what is *not*—within the team to make needed adjustments.[12] But that means that leaders need to be open to employees' input and communicate with them.

Leader trust affects the team and organizational performance because employees are more willing to carry out the leader's tasks and strategies, suspend questions or doubts about the team, and work toward a joint team goal.[13] This type of cooperation between employees improves the overall performance and productivity of the team. Also, when employees work together and increase their performance, they are working together better. They are also more satisfied performing their job duties, affecting the overall environment within the department and organization.

Overall, research shows that when leaders create a trusting environment within their team, employees feel safer and are more loyal to the organization, resulting in increased communication, sharing of knowledge, productivity, and cooperation.[14] These variables lead to increased overall job satisfaction and decreased intention to leave.

The examples provided show the positive benefits to a team and organization when employees trust their leaders. However, we know that things are not always positive. Employees who do not have a trusting relationship with their leader will negatively impact the team and organization.

Negative Implications

Most people can probably think of a situation where they didn't trust their leader. I have spoken to frustrated employees who felt let down because their leader didn't back them up when confronted with a situation and, instead, threw their employees under the bus. I have also spoken to employees whose leaders speak negatively about them or their team, leaving them no confidence in their leader.

Employees who have little trust in their leader are likely to exhibit high turnover intention and reduced knowledge-sharing behavior because of their lack of resources and confidence in their leader.[15] In opposition to relationships with high trust, leaders who don't have trusting relationships will see lower productivity and cooperation from their employees.

Employees who do not trust their leaders tend to focus on nonproductive issues such as self-protection, which leads to negative attitudes and lower job-related performance accordingly.[16]

For example, how often have you seen employees act out or focus on menial things because they don't like or trust their leader? In addition, healthcare research has shown that nurses who lack trust in their leaders have higher medication errors, decreased patient care, and increased safety issues.[17] Unfortunately, when employees lack trust and act out in healthcare situations, the negative results may impact patients.

If trust is lacking, people may even withhold information that would hinder the flow of information and could diminish performance. In addition, people are prone to lie when trust is not present.[18] I have seen employees refuse to train new employees or sit there and watch someone do something wrong and not say a word. The negative implications of a lack of trust in a department or organization can be catastrophic. If a leader is unaware of what is going on in their area, satisfaction and morale will continue to decrease, and people will ultimately leave.

Whether positive or negative, leaders must understand the types of relationships they have with their employees and be aware of what is going on within their areas. They truly need to establish trust with employees, and it is up to the leader to maintain that feeling of trust. Research shows the positive implications of high-trust relationships and the detrimental effects of perceived low trust. Therefore, it's in the organization's best interest to help support its leaders and their relationships with employees.

CHAPTER 5
Leader Trust

Key Points

❖ An employee's perception of their leader affects the level of trust the employee perceives.

❖ Employees trust their organizations to keep them safe, pay them for work performed, and have the employee's best interests in mind.

Reflection Questions

❖ How do you handle the situation when an employee brings a concern to you?

❖ Does your team feel that if they bring a concern to you, they can trust you to follow up on it?

CHAPTER 6

Leader Communication

*The most important thing in communication
is hearing what isn't said.*

—BILL GEORGE

I work in a busy dermatology office, and when I came in this morning, I noticed that our schedule was more packed than usual. I asked my coworkers if they knew what was going on, but no one knew. Finally, someone mentioned that she thought she remembered seeing an email a few days ago about one of the other dermatologists having to take an emergency leave, but she couldn't remember the details.

The day was horrible. Patients were upset about the delays and different ways we did things versus their usual office, and we couldn't keep up with the volume of people in the office.

At the end of the day, our manager, Donna, stopped in and asked why she had received several patient complaints that day. I explained that it was a busy day, and we couldn't keep up with the volume and had struggles with patients coming from another office. Donna looked at me confused and said, "I sent you an email on Monday telling you that Dr. Jay was out unexpectedly and that his patients were being put on other schedules for a few days instead of canceling them all. I told you all this was happening; I don't understand why you were unaware. You all know you have to check your email, so there is no excuse for the patients' complaints." I looked at her and said, "We are busy and short-staffed; we don't get to check our email much."

IN ADDITION TO LEADER SUPPORT AND TRUST, COMMUNICATION is another significant part of perceived leader support. Communication is a constant topic and always seems to arise when discussing improving employee relations. Leaders often ask, "What types of communication are appropriate to share, and how does a leader navigate their way through knowing what to communicate and what not to?"

Especially during tough and unprecedented times, employees look to their leaders and organization to communicate. Whether to communicate a current plan of action or an organization's understanding of tough times, leaders need communication to help staff feel connected and informed. Communication is essential to a team, and good communication skills can affect the climate of a team.[1] In addition, communication helps provide employees with details about their work and a sense of their wider work environment.[2] By providing more communication to employees, the goal for leaders is to ensure their employees are aware of the direction the organization is moving.

This chapter discusses leader communication and how it affects employee productivity. Next, I look at communication from the organizational level and what employees want from their organization.

Leader Communication

Research has confirmed that communication is one of the most important tools a leader can use to influence team member performance.[3] The more communication a leader has with their employees, the better employees will perform. Excellent and consistent communication is a leader's tool that lays the initial leadership foundation for team dynamics.[4]

For example, hospitals receive their Hospital Consumer Assessment of Healthcare Providers and Systems (HCAHPS) survey results, which are surveys of patients' perspectives of hospital care they received. HCAHPS is critical to healthcare providers because they show the patients' perspective of the care they received. In addition, leaders should discuss their department's results with their team. This way, employees know and understand the areas in which they are doing well and the areas that need improvement.

For a leader, meeting with your team is an opportunity to openly discuss the results, address the areas that need improvement, and develop goals to improve. I have seen some leaders who communicate incredibly well; they interact with their team and bring their team together to develop a plan of action. I have also seen other leaders who take the HCAHPS results and post them in the staff breakroom with a note for all staff to read. However, employees may not understand or even look at the results without communication from their leader. They will not know where improvement opportunities exist or their progress toward the organization's goals. Two different examples with two different teams, and you can probably guess which team saw improvement and which team struggled.

Effective leader communication provides clear direction for the team as it works toward organizational goals and expectations[5] that enhance team performance.[6]

For example, many teams have a daily huddle at the beginning of their shifts. Healthcare organizations understand that collective learning occurs through group social interactions, and daily huddles are an avenue for collaborative learning. Huddles are an excellent way for teams to communicate different things that are going on, address any issues that may come up, and develop a plan for the day.[7]

For example, we used to have a daily leadership huddle for all leaders to discuss anything going on within the organization. Then leaders were expected to take any pertinent information from those huddles back to their teams. These huddles allowed leaders to connect and obtain information about different things at different levels within the organization, and leaders took that information back to their employees.

Leader communication does not always mean communication as a group. I told the story of the leader who was so busy on his phone when an employee was trying to speak to him that the employee just walked away. I have had employees tell me that they have not seen their leader in weeks, and unless they need something, they *won't* see them. I have other leaders who will only communicate with their employees through text or email but leave it up to them to check for anything new. My question in these areas is how does the leader know what is going on with their team? My answer is they don't unless someone tells them or something happens that makes them aware. And then, I know many leaders who communicate daily, in person, with their employees. These leaders talk with their employees as things come up and work in the "trenches" with their teams. Predictable and timely communication helps develop interpersonal relationships with team members, positively affecting their performance.[8] In addition, these leaders are aware of the everyday challenges they face. Employees who have this type of high communication with their leaders are more motivated because they feel supported.[9] Communication between leader and employee is the key to a high-performing and effective team.

Virtual Communication

Unfortunately, with the COVID-19 pandemic, all in-person meetings stopped, and I think many employees saw a considerable decline in communication from their leaders. Ultimately, the ways leaders were communicating with their teams changed. Daily huddles and meetings with leadership turned into online meetings, and staff meetings ultimately stopped in many areas.

Research indicates that a virtual environment affects relationships between team members and employees' attitudes toward their organization.[10] Due to the change in communication and the lack of face-to-face meetings, the relationships between leaders and employees suffered, as employees felt less connected and informed. In addition, leaders also had employees working remotely, creating a new challenge for communication. Yet, despite the challenges, communication was needed more than ever, so leaders had to be creative and communicate more than they had pre-pandemic. It was up to leaders to recognize and adapt to the new challenges, as more frequent leader communication leads to enhanced leader-team relationship development, greater levels of information exchange, and increased virtual team effectiveness.[11]

For example, I know some leaders who email and text employees with information as they get it. In addition, emailing and texting employees created more avenues for employees to ask questions, which is essential to keeping the lines of communication open. Other leaders put together videos and presentations and sent them to all employees to discuss new procedure changes or to show employees how to use new equipment. Leaders understanding the new challenges of virtual communication was necessary to understand how these changes affected organizational dynamics while maintaining management effectiveness.[12]

Whatever the reason, through the pandemic, leaders saw how imperative it is to stay connected with their teams, whether virtually or not, and leaders had to make communication a priority.

Organizational Communication

Like leader communication, organizational communication affects overall employee satisfaction and perceived support. In addition, research shows that organizational communication provides a sense of comfort for employees when working to create job satisfaction, and it also impacts employee performance.[13]

Organizational communication, to me, is when employees receive communication from higher levels of the organization, not just their direct leader. Employees may know that their leader supports them but may feel that the organization does not. Therefore, organizational leaders should promote a collaborative working culture with open communication to encourage social exchanges.[14] The higher levels of leadership within an organization must be willing to create an environment and culture of communication. If they don't, their leaders won't do it either.

For an organization to be successful, communication is needed to share the organization's goals and objectives. If there is a lack of communication, it can affect the organization's overall objectives.[15] In addition, changes often happen that affect the entire organization, which administrators need to share with their employees. Examples of organizational changes are a change in the employee health record system that an organization uses, a change in the corporate structure, leadership changes, feedback from a regulatory agency survey, and any significant change occurring throughout the organization.

Large organizational changes should come from higher levels within the organization and not just be left for the individual leaders to discuss with their teams. When significant changes are coming, organizations must communicate the reasons for the change and their vision of what the changes will mean for its success. Individual leaders should answer questions and discuss with their teams for further clarification after communication of changes goes out from administration. Still, significant changes should not be left for leaders to announce.

Communication strategies vary by organization. Larger organizations may rely heavily on email communication, whereas smaller organizations may have better results via face-to-face communication. We know that ineffective communication can negatively impact patient outcomes, nursing staff turnover, and healthcare costs, so organizations need to be aware of how and what they communicate.[16]

For example, I have known administrators who walk the organization's floors and have face-to-face interactions with employees. On the other hand, I have also known administrators who don't speak to employees or even leave their executive suites.

In organizations where administrators interact with employees, administrators communicate directly to employees and answer employees' questions. In contrast, in organizations where administrators don't interact with employees, employees have no idea who the administrators are; employees don't get to ask questions, and they may never speak to an administrator. Regardless of the communication channels an organization may use, the communication must be happening, and the employees must receive said communication.

For example, suppose a large organization communicates solely through email and knows that most clinical employees don't check their email. How are the organization's changes and objectives getting through to those employees? Only using one communication method leaves a significant chance that employees are not receiving any or very little organizational communication.

CHAPTER 6
Leader Communication

Key Points

❖ Communication is essential for any organization to be successful.

❖ Communication provides direction toward the overall organizational goals and expectations.

❖ Communication should occur in different ways to ensure employees receive the intended message.

Reflection Questions

❖ How do you communicate with your team?

❖ Do you only use one mode of communication, or do you use several so that you know the message is received?

❖ How does your organization communicate essential information?

Leader & Employee Relationships

The most important single ingredient in the formula of success is knowing how to get along with people.

—THEODORE ROOSEVELT

Mary has worked at Rover Medical Center her entire career of twenty years. She has worked her way up from a graduate nurse to a charge nurse of her unit. She has had many leaders come and go throughout the years and has constantly developed a good relationship with her leaders.

Tiffany, her newest leader, started at Rover a little over six months ago and has been very standoffish with the employees. Mary has been welcoming and has gone to Tiffany to talk to her about the department on several occasions. Mary has also mentioned different concerns and ideas for things that have occurred. However, Tiffany has not been receptive to any ideas that Mary—or any other staff—presents and has no interest in hearing ways the department can improve.

Tiffany doesn't interact with her employees much and uses a very standoffish approach if she does. Because of the limited interactions, staff don't trust Tiffany, nor do they feel any support from her.

As the previous chapters have shown, employees who feel they have leader support, trust, and communication will positively affect the organization. In addition, leader support will affect the relationships that leaders have with their employees, which are critical in determining the effectiveness of a team.

When considering the relationships between a leader and an employee, I refer to the leader-member exchange (LMX) theory. This leadership theory is one that I relate to and genuinely enjoy due to its strong emphasis on the leader and employee, their relationships, and how they directly affect the organization.

As a leader, do I believe that only one leadership style works? Of course not. And I feel that all leaders have their own styles that make them successful. However, when it comes to leader support, I feel that the LMX theory provides insights on relationship building that can have extremely positive implications for both leaders and organizations.

This chapter will briefly overview the LMX theory and the implications of both high- and low-quality relationships, followed by the organizational implications of LMX relationships.

LMX Relationships

The LMX theory focuses on the relationship between leaders and employees and on developing mature leadership relationships.[1]

The LMX theory brings attention to the entire leadership process by focusing on the dyadic relationship between the leader and the employee.[2] If these relationships are effective, they will benefit both parties.[3]

For example, research shows that the leader-member relationship is critical to the employee's development when an employee is new to an organization.[4] A lot of focus has been on employee onboarding programs within the last few years. Unfortunately, as much as human resources professionals focus on onboarding, employees often get to their department, and that "welcoming" feeling disappears quickly. I have seen numerous situations in which employees never even hear from their leader during their first week in orientation, so they have no idea where to report or even what their schedule is. I have also seen where an employee reports to their designated area, and staff are so busy that they have no idea what to do with the employee, and the leader is not there. For this reason, it is *so* critical that leaders begin the development of those relationships immediately.

As relationships develop between leaders and employees, leaders are more likely to focus on employees they feel can grow within the organization, take on more demanding work assignments, and provide support toward their development, developing high-quality relationships.[5]

Research shows that leader-member relationships develop over time through a series of interactions between leaders and employees.[6] As a leader, the more I know how my employee works and interacts, the more I can determine the type of relationship the employee may want. Many benefits come from positive relationships between leader and employee, which benefit the organization, the leader, and the employee.

Several factors can affect the relationship between a leader and an employee. The level of mutual trust, loyalty, influence on one another, competence, and perceived equity of the relationship can all influence the relationship.[7] A high-quality relationship develops when the relationship meets both parties' levels of expectation.[8] The employees in these relationships are more compatible, have better relations with the leader, and match the leader's style of implicit leadership.[9,10]

As a leader, I highly encourage leaders to take the time when interviewing someone to see if they are compatible with your style. We all have different leadership styles and personalities, so behavioral-based interviews are good because they show how the employee may react in various situations.

Behavior-based interviewing is a technique used by employers to allow a job candidate to demonstrate their potential for succeeding in the organization by providing specific examples of how they handled specific situations in their past. These scenarios can help give a leader insight into the behavior and personality of the employee.

For example, asking a candidate how they handled a high-stress situation or a situation with a challenging coworker can give a leader some insight into how they handle themselves under pressure. Also, how employees answer may give the leader insight into whether the employee looks to grow within the organization and sees potential growth opportunities.

Not all relationships are the same, and some employees have no desire to have a high-quality relationship with their leader. And, vice versa, a leader may not want to have a relationship with some of their employees. However, most employees seek a high-quality relationship with their leader, affecting job satisfaction and retention.

Research shows that leaders are best poised for success when they know their relationships with their employees.[11] A leader may not want to understand what types of relationships their employees want. However, the positive implications of high-quality relationships far outweigh the negative ones.

Implications of High-Quality Relationships

Most leaders could probably name their employees with whom they would consider having a high-quality relationship. In high-quality relationships, the leader values employees and encourages the success of those employees they value most.[12]

Characteristics of high-quality relationships include mutual trust, respect, and influence.[13] In addition, these high-quality relationships typically develop when leaders assign more exciting tasks, initiate more exchanges, provide access to essential resources, give employees increased autonomy and responsibilities, and establish closer relationships.[14,15] These employees are whom leaders trust to get their work done and don't worry that they are doing something they're not supposed to do. The relationship between leader and employee is at a level where there are no questions about loyalty or support, and the leadership between members is exceptionally high.[16] This high-quality relationship bonds the leader and employee to exceed the traditional work relationship and effectively accomplish the organization's goals.[17]

When I was new to the human resources field, I developed a high-quality relationship with my leader. We had mutual trust and respect for one another and developed a solid, high-quality relationship over time. She influenced me and helped shape me into the leader I am today.

Leaders who develop relationships with their employees help reduce job insecurity, stress, and emotional exhaustion, resulting in decreased turnover.[18] I know that I can think of areas where the leader has a higher-quality relationship with their employees and the difference in employee relation issues versus those where the leader does not have high-quality relationships. Additionally, leaders will see how the quality of their relationships with their staff is related to productivity, satisfaction, and employee turnover[19, 20] by seeing the effects on employee productivity in those with whom they have a relationship.

Research shows that LMX high-quality relationships are interpersonal relationships characterized by high levels of influence and liking, leading to increased satisfaction and commitment to the leader, employee, and the organization.[21]

For example, many studies show examples of increased productivity and satisfaction over time in organizations that foster high-quality relationships with employees.

Higher-quality LMX relationships are related to better job performance, higher overall satisfaction, more commitment, better communication, less role conflict, more role clarity, the competence of leaders and employees, and less intention to quit.[22] In addition, high-quality employees will accept feedback and try harder to meet the leader's expectations, resulting in increased productivity.[23]

For example, you can probably think of which of your employees will take constructive feedback and improve their performance instead of just hearing what you have to say and not changing anything. In connection with job satisfaction, research also shows that employees will have a high-quality relationship with their leader when using their strengths in their work environment.[24] As a leader, if I recognize my employees' strengths and place them in positions where they can use them, they will be more satisfied and look to grow further within their role and the organization.

Something that can happen within a department where a leader has both high- and low-quality relationships is the employees who have low-quality relationships may feel there is strong favoritism between the leader and employees who have those high-quality relationships. Morale and team dynamics will be affected if leaders allow favoritism to enter into the equation. Hence, leaders need to be aware of the different relationships with their employees.

Implications of Low-Quality Relationships

Characteristics of low-quality relationships within an LMX relationship are low trust, respect, and obligation, and employees only do what their job description requires.[25] A low-quality relationship doesn't mean that the leader is mean or disrespectful to employees. On the contrary, leaders treat their low-quality relationships fairly but rely on formal authority and give no particular attention to these employees.[26, 27] Also, even though the relationship may not be as good between leader and employee, employees may not be any less satisfied with the leader or their influence.[28] Furthermore, the employees in low-quality relationships base their exchanges directly specified by their job description, nothing more.[29]

I have had several conversations with employees who are content with coming to work and doing their job—again—nothing more. They do not get involved in the drama or care about taking on anything more than their current role. And nothing is wrong with that. If a leader treats these employees fairly, then someone in a low-quality relationship may choose to stay with the organization and be happy with the relationship status with their leader. As stated earlier, it is a choice by both parties to determine the amount of effort to exert into the relationship.

Research shows that low-quality employees are not necessarily low performers; instead, they may not perceive a high-quality relationship as worth their effort.[30] Also, research shows that if a leader works hard and is authentic in their actions, then the otherwise negative connotations associated with low-quality relationships are nonexistent.[31] Therefore, an LMX model allows employees with different expectations to decide which type of relationship best suits their needs.

Regardless of your leadership style, it would be best to recognize your high versus low employees as a leader. By recognizing the needs and wants of employees, leaders can work with employees' strengths for the benefit of the employee, leader, and organization.

Organizational Implications

Researchers saw the potential and opportunities for organizations to gain valuable insight into different organizational functions by encouraging leader and employee relations across the different organizational levels.[32] Researchers felt that organizations need differentiated relationships at the organizational level because those relationships form a broader, more constructive system.[33] Organizations are more substantial and diversified when they have different relationship levels throughout their departments.

For example, LMX encourages leadership relationships among peers, teammates, and across organizational levels to build stronger bonds throughout the organization.[34] By managing those high-quality relationships, leaders affect critical organizational outcomes because the leader and employee relationships are critical factors for socialization and reducing employee stress and turnover.[35] However, strong bonds also develop between the high- and low-quality relationship employees. Therefore, the patterns of relationship quality within the leadership structure are critical for the organization to watch, specifically looking at those task-oriented, low-quality relationships and how the different relationships affect the leader and the entire organization.[36]

For example, suppose a leader has more low-quality relationships. In that case, the organization could see low productivity and job satisfaction versus leaders with high-quality relationships. By examining the relationships among leaders, an organization should see those leaders who develop relationships with their staff and those who focus on other areas. Based on the organizational goals, they can determine where they need to place specific leaders.

The different LMX relationships within departments may create unequal status perceptions and psychological boundaries that lead to different interests and expectations.[37] However, it is best that leaders focus on both groups, regardless of high or low, and look for different ways to build trust and respect with all employees, in turn, building a stronger team. Due to these correlations, we see why the relationship process of the LMX model is critical between a leader, an employee, and the organization.

CHAPTER 7

Leader & Employee Relationships

Key Points

* The LMX theory focuses on the relationships between leaders and employees.

* Mutual trust, loyalty, and influence determine the level of the relationship.

* Leaders should have both high-quality and low-quality relationships.

Reflection Questions

* What type of relationships do you have with your employees?

* Can you identify your employees with whom you could have high-quality relationships? And those that you could have low-quality relationships?

* Does your organization value the different relationships with employees?

Strategies to Improve Feelings of Leader Support

As a collaborative leader, you support people in their work—you
remove roadblocks and help them win.

—KENNETH H. BLANCHARD

Darcy is a manager in a busy nursing unit. Recognition is
something that Darcy prioritizes, and she finds diverse
ways to identify her staff and let them know she appreciates their hard work.

When Darcy got this job, she noticed how her staff
were surprised to see her out on the floor and even
more surprised when she would give accolades when she
would see something good. Darcy does not do anything
extreme but instead vows to make it a priority to ensure
that the staff knows they are appreciated.

One day, when a staff member called off sick, and
Darcy called in one of her other employees, Darcy gave
the employee that came in a bag of her favorite candy and
a handwritten thank-you note. A simple act of kindness
that did not take long to prepare, but it was an act that
meant a lot to the staff member that came in because
they felt appreciated.

EVERY TEAM IS DIFFERENT AND REQUIRES A UNIQUE LEVEL OF support. Therefore, for a leader to improve feelings of support on their team, they must understand what their team wants for support. As discussed in chapter 4, leader support helps staff retention, productivity, and morale. It also adds value and awareness to the team. A supportive leader involves everyone and sees all employees as a critical part of the team.[1]

To find out what your team needs, you must *talk* to them. Ask them how you can support them and what they need from you. Take the time. You will have those employees who do not want anything from you, who want to come to work, do their job, and go home. Then you will have those other employees who desire more attention from you and need more from you to feel supported.

In this chapter, I discuss different strategies for leaders to improve the support they show for their teams through recognition, addressing employee concerns and more. I then discuss different things Lauren, the manager from chapter 4, can do to support your team.

The Need for Employee Recognition

It is good to ask your employees how they like to be recognized. We know that employees want to feel valued; they want their efforts recognized somehow. But some employees do not want public recognition, while others want everyone to know of their achievements. Part of supporting your employees and valuing them is understanding what makes them comfortable.

By valuing and supporting your employees, you, as a leader, can reduce job difficulties and increase job satisfaction.[2] In addition, research shows that nonmonetary recognition has higher motivational effects than monetary recognition.[3]

Recognition can be as easy as sending a quick note to an employee saying "excellent job" or by giving a shout-out to an employee during a team huddle. Receiving acknowledgment and credit from a leader for excellent work often surpasses monetary reward or elevation in status.[4] However, the point of recognition is to show that you recognize their effort and value what they do as their leader. It needs to mean something, so let them know you appreciate them when you know one of your employees goes the extra mile or deals with a tricky situation.

Especially during tough times like staffing shortages or a pandemic, a simple thank you to your employees can go a long way. A simple action such as bringing their favorite candy bar or leaving them a little something on their computer can mean a lot. The trivial things sound silly, and will they solve all your employee issues? Of course not! But can they help your employees feel supported during a tough time? Recognizing your employees at least shows them you are there.

There are many different ways you, as a leader, can appreciate your staff: through email, a personal handwritten note, a keepsake, or verbal appreciation. The recognition should show your employees that you value what they do. In addition, you need to try to acknowledge your employees often, not just when something big happens. Frequently tangibly demonstrating appreciation for your employees lets them know that you engage in the department's daily activities and are aware of what is happening within the department.

Addressing Employee Concerns

As mentioned in chapter 4, a leader cannot just ignore an employee's concerns hoping the complaints will disappear.

If an employee brings a concern to their leader, it matters to them, that means that a leader cannot just ignore it. I have had employees who need to talk something out and have someone listen to them. Yes, we are all busy and have things we need to do, but to take the time to sit down with an employee and listen to their concerns could save you time in the future when a more significant problem occurs. If an employee brings a concern to their leader about another employee, a leader needs to follow up on the concern and let the employee know they will investigate the concern. But the leader needs to examine the situation, address any issues, and not just push things off. Issues may include conflicting personalities or poor job performance.

As a leader, if you do not know how to address the issues, then get human resources or your leader involved, but do not just let the issue fester because it will worsen. If the leader does not address the issue or the employee does not feel their leader will not address it, the leader may lose good employees.

Additional Support

Leaders can support their employees in a number of different ways, more than showing recognition, making employees feel valued and addressing their concerns. These few things are some of the easiest for leaders to do, but, as stated earlier, leaders need to know what their team needs from them.

Another action leaders can take is to be visible to their employees. When the department is busy, and staff is spread thin, leaders can show their support by collaborating with their staff and helping them in times of need, whether it be taking a patient assignment, helping with meds, or helping with patient rounds. When staff sees their leaders in the trenches with them, they feel supported, making all the difference.

As a team leader, your staff looks to you for many things, including strength and inspiration, especially in challenging times. Another way a leader can show their support is by empowering and inspiring their employees. In addition, a leader naturally motivates their team by giving everyone an equal shot at opportunities, promotions, assignments, and training.[5] Finally, leaders' support and understanding can enforce employees' positive perception of leadership behaviors, and, in return, employees will devote more to their work.[6] Overall, employees need to feel their leaders support them, and the more support employees feel, the more employees will give back to the organization.

Leaders Making Excuses

Leaders' support is essential for employees' job satisfaction, especially in extraordinary situations like economic crises or pandemics.[7] Unfortunately, sometimes leaders find it easier to make excuses for allowing bad behavior than to confront the problem. Due to being short-staffed, I have also seen leaders make excuses for employees' bad behavior because they do not want to eliminate the employee. However, by putting up with the behavior, the leader is not showing support to all the other employees who witness the bad behavior. Employees tell me that they would sooner work short rather than put up with someone's attitude or poor job performance. As a result of leaders not addressing the issue, employees feel ignored or that the leader does not care, affecting job satisfaction. Job satisfaction is essential in maintaining an experienced and skilled workforce and leads to higher productivity, increased communication, and better cooperation with coworkers and leaders.[8] The last thing a leader wants is for job satisfaction to decrease due to employees' lousy behavior, which negatively affects the rest of the team.

Leaders need to understand and realize the perception it gives when they do not address employee concerns and how it can negatively affect the whole team. When a leader does not address a concern, employees may perceive that the leader does not care.

Revisiting Lauren

Let us revisit chapter 4 and the manager, Lauren. Lauren's staff has grown incredibly frustrated with the lack of support they feel from her. Lauren's staff rarely see her walk through the department, check on them, or offer them help. Instead, many staff see Lauren sitting in her office throughout the day and leaving early, without even glancing their way.

Sadly, this story may not be far off from things you have experienced. Hopefully, as leaders, you understand Lauren's staff's perceptions and frustrations. I can hear people saying that Lauren may have had meetings to attend or had administrative things she had to complete. And I agree, a leader's staff does not always know the things that leaders have to take care of throughout the day—saying that it all comes down to perception. But, in this case, all Lauren's staff wanted was for Lauren to acknowledge them and for Lauren to show she cared that they were busy.

I know of organizations that will not schedule meetings on certain days or after certain hours so that leaders can have time to spend in their departments. But, again, in this case, Lauren should have taken the time to pull her staff together and quickly check on them or be present in the department to see what help she could lend. Even if it was just for short periods between meetings, she still should have still been present for her staff. To leave at five without even checking in with her staff is not the behavior of a supportive leader, and it is no wonder that Lauren's department had a problem retaining staff members.

The following chapters will further discuss support by expanding on trust, communication, and leader-employee relationships and additional strategies for leaders to improve support in these areas.

CHAPTER 8
Strategies to Improve Feelings of Leadership

Key Strategies

❖ Recognize your employees in a variety of ways.

❖ Take the time to address your employees' concerns.

❖ Be visible!

❖ Empower and inspire your team!

❖ Do not make excuses for employees' bad behavior.

Reflection Questions

❖ Of the strategies presented, which could you implement with your staff to provide leader support?

❖ Do you find yourself excusing bad behavior instead of confronting the issue?

CHAPTER 9

Strategies to Improve Leader Trust

Don't be afraid to show your vulnerability.
Be transparent with your team, even when the truth
may be unpopular or inconvenient.

—BILL GEORGE

Several times throughout the week, Jason's staff brings different concerns to him. Whether the concerns be about equipment or resources needed, concerns about procedures, or issues between staff members, Jason, the ICU manager, hears them all. And he prioritizes ensuring that he follows up with his team members in person as often as possible.

For example, one of Jason's night shift nursing assistants brought a concern to Jason's attention regarding the night shift running low on blankets at night and not being able to get more supplies, as the warehouse closes at 6 p.m. Jason told the staff member that he would see what he could do and get back to her in a few days.

Jason spoke with the materials management manager to see what options were available without going too far over their allotted par level of blankets. After discussing a few different options, the managers decided that the best option would be to allow ICU to have a backup supply of blankets available in the department. To ensure these blankets did not "wander off" during the day shift, Jason agreed to keep them in his office so they would not get counted with the rest of the supply.

Jason met with his night crew that evening and told them about the new process with the blankets. A simple solution and quick turnaround helped show Jason's night shift team that he heard their concern and found a quick solution.

CHAPTER 8 DISCUSSED STRATEGIES THAT LEADERS CAN TAKE TO improve perceived employee support. These strategies include recognizing team members, addressing employee concerns, being visible, empowering and inspiring your team, and not excusing lousy employee behavior.

This chapter will add to your toolbox by discussing different strategies leaders can use to build and improve perceived trust within their teams. We will also revisit Brandon, our manager from chapter 5, who gossiped with other staff members about his night shift team instead of following through on an employee concern. So we will see what strategies Brandon should use to regain his team members' trust.

With tight staffing and employees having to work short-staffed, higher-acuity patients, and staff burnout, employees need to trust that their leader will be there to support them and work alongside them. As discussed in chapter 5, if team members trust their leader, it will result in many positive implications for the organization. Understanding that a leader's primary means of influence comes through trust[1] means that having strategies to develop trust is critical. However, as critical as trust is to a leader-employee relationship, trust is not an easy feat for a leader to achieve. Employees look to their leaders to be an example, exhibit compassion when communicating, help when needed, and follow through on what they say, all while being authentic in their behavior. However, nothing is more damaging than a lack of trust between leaders and their employees, so the leader and organization must ensure that they build trust.[2]

Leaders can use different strategies to build perceived trust within their department, and we will look at a few of those strategies next.

Be Present and Authentic

There is a lot of research about leadership and different leadership styles, but what characteristics help a leader with trust? When you think of different leaders you have had and their difference in characteristics, I can almost guarantee that the leaders who showed compassion, humility, and empathy were the ones you trusted the most. The more a leader shows interest in their employees and their employees' feelings, the more likely that an employee will feel they can trust their leader.

Of course, everyone is busy, and some days a leader may not have the time, energy, or patience to take time with their staff. But as a leader, you must show your employees that you care; you need to be present when they talk to you, and you need to respond in a way that shows compassion. So, on your less busy days, you need to try to be present within your department. Different ways to be present in your department may be little things like being at the nurse's station and fielding phone calls or asking your staff what they need as they pass by. You can also walk the floor and check in on patients and staff as they are busy walking in and out of rooms.

In addition, leaders need to be authentic when interacting with their staff. A leader who genuinely wants to help and interact with their staff builds a more trusting environment than those leaders who may help their team without being sincere.[3] And do not think that your team will not know if you don't want to be there or if you help for five minutes then disappear back to your office. If you do not want to help, then do not pretend to! But also do not wonder why your team does not trust you to help when they need you. Your team will know from past experiences that they cannot rely on you, as you will either disappear after a short time or you really don't want to be there to begin with.

Leader Follow-Through

I know of leaders who try to appease everyone, so when you call them about a concern, they always tell you they will investigate it or put someone right on it. Yet the problem does not get fixed, and the leader has no follow-through. On the other hand, a leader who follows through to make sure the job gets done right enjoys the added benefit of building stronger relationships of trust among their employees and peers.[4] Leaders show more credibility to their team and peers and earn more trust when they follow through on what they say. Additionally, a credible leader will be honest and say they must first investigate the issue but will get back to you, and they actually do. I wholeheartedly admit that when I do not know the answer, I let my staff or peers know that I will investigate it and get back to them within a certain amount of time.

As leaders, we do not have to know everything, but we need to be able to admit that we do not know and know what resources we must find to get the answers we need. As a leader, if employees come to you and, more times than not, you do not get back to them or help with their concerns, they will stop asking and feel it is worthless to bring anything to you moving forward, as it has not benefited them in the past. They will lose that trust.

Ask Questions & Grow Your Team

A leader who is interested in what their team members are experiencing or what staff need shows they care. I ask my team members what I can do to help make their job easier or help take some stress off. A leader who can step in and help when staff need an extra hand is a leader who builds a trusting relationship with their team. The leader must show that it is okay to ask questions, ask for help, or ask what is needed. Leaders who create an environment where it is safe to ask questions foster trust within their department. Questions often help to encourage the exchange of valuable and essential information among team members, and by encouraging team members to ask questions, leaders help build trust.[5] Also, by encouraging employees to ask questions, a leader can see areas where staff may need extra training or new areas in which they want to learn.

I am the type of leader who enjoys helping my team grow and furthering their career. Leaders who are compassionate enough to teach employees the necessary knowledge to conduct tasks while also allowing them time and space to learn build trust among their team.[6] Leaders must help and encourage their employees to grow into their roles and grow beyond their roles if they so desire. Too often, leaders will not share their knowledge with staff due to being afraid that someone will take their job. This type of behavior also creates distrust, as employees feel they do not have all the information they need to do their job. So employees feel stuck at a certain level, get bored, and move on over time.

Stop Gossip

Gossip is present in any environment where multiple people are working. However, a culture of respect and trust nurtures an environment and team that will not tolerate gossip.[7]

A leader who participates in the gossip only makes the situation worse. Leaders who avoid gossiping and instead help eliminate it from the workplace conversations demonstrate humility and respect for others, allowing trust to grow.[8]

Instead of entertaining the gossip, a leader needs to understand why the gossip is happening.

For example, if the gossip is about the organization, are team members assuming things because they miss crucial communication? Or because no one will listen to their concerns about a particular subject?

If the gossip is about things happening within the department or organization, then the leader needs to address what they can and discourage any harmful discussions.[9] The main objective is to stop the gossip and not participate in it.

Improving communication, which we will discuss in the next chapter, can significantly diminish gossip about things happening within the organization. Usually, a leader can identify where the gossip originates or from whom it originates. Then, as a leader, it is imperative to confront these team members and explain the problem and its impact on the team.[10]

Hopefully, by addressing the gossip and hearing the concerns of your team, you can put their worries at ease and stop the gossip from becoming more hostile. And, if the gossip is not about work and instead about a person, the leader must address the team immediately. Additionally, by addressing the gossip, the leader shows that they will not tolerate such behavior in the department and organization. Finally, as a leader, it is imperative to lead by example by not participating in any gossip and addressing it when the gossip arises.

Revisiting Brandon

Revisiting Brandon, our manager from chapter 5, we know Brandon's issues are a lack of follow-up to his night charge nurse, gossip about his night shift team members, and not leading by example, all of which have caused a lack of trust with his staff. So what should Brandon have done differently?

As a manager, if he did not know whether the concern brought to him was legitimate, then the first thing he should have done was stay later a few days and see how the day shift staff is leaving their rooms at the end of the shift. Brandon can then directly address his day shift staff instead of feeling that someone is just complaining. However, a charge nurse is a leadership role, so Brandon should be able to trust that any concerns brought to him are legitimate and are things that he should address.

As a leader, Brandon should never tell a staff member that another member is complaining about them, since doing so could result in a hostile work relationship and gossip between his employees. For Brandon to gain back the trust of his night shift, he will have to show more follow-through on addressing issues and be more present. I know leaders who would work a night shift a couple of times a month just to be in contact with their staff and see potential areas of need. It also shows employees that the leader cares enough to take the initiative to be present when the employees need them, not just when it is convenient for the leader.

Trust is not an easy thing to get back once it is gone. However, if Brandon takes the steps to intentionally show he cares and shows he can be there and be supportive of his entire team, he will hopefully regain the trust of his staff over time.

CHAPTER 9

Strategies to Improve Leader Trust

Key Strategies

- ❖ Be present and authentic.
- ❖ Follow through with things brought to your attention.
- ❖ Ask and encourage questions.
- ❖ Help your staff members grow!
- ❖ Do not allow an environment of gossip.

Reflection Questions

- ❖ Of the presented strategies, in what areas do you feel you can improve?
- ❖ Would your team say that you lead by example?

Strategies to Improve Leader Communication

Developing excellent communication skills is absolutely essential to effective leadership. The leader must be able to share knowledge and ideas to transmit a sense of urgency and enthusiasm to others. If a leader can't get a message across clearly and motivate others to act on it, then having a message doesn't even matter.

—Gilbert Amelio

At her morning meeting, Michelle, the registration leader, hears that patients coming in for lab work will need to register through the emergency room registration area instead of the regular registration area at the front of the hospital due to a construction project starting Monday. Signage will be placed outside the hospital to inform patients of the change and give directions to the other entrance.

At the end of the meeting, Michelle went back to her department and pulled her team together to make sure they knew. Michelle tells them what is happening and assures them that the staff members at lab registration will move to the ER to account for the additional patients the staff will see.

Michelle met with her day shift team face-to-face but stays later that night to inform her night shift team. Michelle also follows up by sending her entire team an email with the information about the temporary process change and the estimated length of time things will be different.

CHAPTER 8 GAVE STRATEGIES FOR LEADERS TO IMPROVE SUPPORT by implementing such things as recognizing team members, addressing employee concerns, being visible to staff, empowering and inspiring staff, and not excusing poor behavior. Next, chapter 9 gave strategies for improving leader trust, including leaders being present and authentic, following through on employee questions and concerns, encouraging and asking questions, helping staff members grow, and creating an environment that does not support or allow for gossip. Finally, chapter 10 will add to this list by giving leaders strategies to improve communication with their team.

After looking at different strategies to improve communication, we will reexamine the chapter 6 manager, Donna, who communicates strictly through email to her staff. The staff cannot read their email due to being busy and short-staffed, so we will look at ways she can communicate to ensure the staff gets the information they need.

Understanding Your Audience

Research tells us that leaders who communicate in various ways through inclusion, collaboration, and regard tend to convey their humility to those around them, which helps build trust with others.[1] When communicating, a leader must know their audience and be able to communicate in a way the audience will understand.

For example, when speaking to someone who does not have a clinical background, a clinical leader must be able to speak in a way that person will understand the message the leader is trying to convey. So, instead of using clinical terms like "intramuscular injection," a leader may say "a shot in the arm."

Silly example, but the point is, if a leader understands who they are speaking to and can understand how to communicate their message in a way the receiver will understand, it shows the leader cares to understand their audience. Additionally, it shows leaders care enough to make sure the message is heard and understood by their team.

Understanding your audience also includes knowing what types of communication work best for them.

For example, is the expectation of communicating with every one of your staff members in person a realistic expectation when a leader has numerous employees on different shifts or even various locations? Is communicating through email the best tool to use when an organization knows that staff does not have ample opportunities to check email regularly?

For a leader, it is critical to understand what your team experiences so you can better navigate the best way to ensure communication is reaching them. The communication processes are the fundamental underlying mechanisms for establishing trust.[2] If a leader takes the time to understand and develop different communication processes for their teams, the more the team will perceive effective open communication. In addition, open and prompt communication among members is an essential characteristic of trusting relationships.[3] So the more open and prompt a leader is with communication, the more trusting relationships they will create with their team.

Different Communication Methods

Understanding your audience means finding the most efficient ways to communicate with your team. The challenge most leaders face is selecting the most productive communication approach to ensure staff members receive and understand the message.[4]

For example, communicating strictly through email may be the most effective way to share a message with your staff in an office environment. However, in a patient care area, as in chapter 6, clinical staff may not have an opportunity to check their email regularly, resulting in staff missing important messages.

Another method many leaders use to communicate is through group text messages. Text messages are an excellent way to keep people in the loop as things are happening. However, there are a few things to keep in mind with group text messages. As a leader, if you are going to communicate with your staff through group text messages, it is your responsibility to ensure that the information you are sharing is appropriate and professional. Staff also need to understand that they are responding to a group and that they also need to be appropriate and professional. Leaders need to make sure to let their staff know that communication may happen through text or email to keep them informed, but there is no expectation for them to reply if they are not working. I have had staff members get upset that their leader sends text messages when they are off the clock, and either they do not want to deal with work outside of work, or they turn their phone off and then feel like they may get in trouble since they did not respond. Also, from the standpoint of human resources, you want to make sure your hourly employees are not doing any work while off the clock.

Email and text messages are an easy way to communicate with staff; however, keep in mind that the number of messages received daily may be overwhelming, so these methods of communication should be in addition to traditional methods of communication.[5]

For example, an in-person conversation can help a leader ensure that their message is clear and understood, whereas a sender does not know how staff receives the message when sent through email or text. Therefore, the time a leader spends time with staff talking and answering questions only improves their understanding of the message. Even after a face-to-face meeting or phone conversation, a follow-up email is a great way to get your message out there again, as staff may have missed something the first time.

Another way a leader may communicate is by putting an informational poster in the break room or at the nurse's station. I knew leaders who would type up minutes from their daily leader meetings and put them in a book. Then, when they returned to work, employees who were off that day had to initial off on those minutes, stating they read them.

Department and organizational newsletters are great ways to get information out to the staff and ensure everyone is receiving the same message. But overall, as a leader, you must understand how to effectively relay the information you have to your team while also understanding how others interpret your message.

Providing Positive and Negative Feedback

Another strategy to help leaders communicate is providing feedback to their staff. Leaders who provide feedback help cultivate feelings of trust among their teams.[6] Feedback may include discussions about an employee's performance or happenings within the department. In addition, chapter 6 discusses how influential leaders communicate with their teams about what is going on within the organization, not just in their department. Employees can trust their leaders more when leaders convey feedback from meetings where feedback affects the department processes and shows the leader's intentions for improving the organization, not just for themselves.[7]

For example, during a morning meeting, the leaders discussed improving patient flow for cardiac patients presenting to the emergency room. After the meeting, the ER director made sure to return to their department and inform their staff of the new process. In addition, the leader made sure to include all their staff in the communication and took feedback on how the process change would positively impact the organization.

Finally, seeking feedback helps leaders understand whether messages have been received and understood.[8] A leader can answer any questions while listening to how the staff interprets the communication and ensures the accuracy of the messaging by spending time with staff. When staff better understand what a leader is communicating, they can better develop an effective plan to implement any necessary changes.[9] In addition to giving feedback from meetings, feedback can include speaking with individual staff members about their performance, attitude, or other positive and negative attributes.

A leader who provides feedback shows others that their growth and development are significant enough to take the time to share feedback with them, conveying both unselfishness and a sense of humility to employees.[10] In addition, whether positive or negative, providing feedback enables leaders to foster trusting relationships with others.

For example, a leader who takes the time to work with an employee struggling in a specific area shows the leader's investment in wanting the employee to grow.

Finally, open, honest conversations with staff help identify any issues within the team and the entire work environment.[11]

For example, when a leader spends time with their staff, it may become apparent that several employees are struggling with a new machine and that more education is needed. Without being open or giving feedback, a leader may not know that staff is struggling.

Additional Ways to Improve Communication

In addition to the above strategies, a leader needs to guarantee an environment where their staff feel safe and empowered to communicate.

For example, having an open-door policy promotes trust and allows staff to address concerns directly while also helping their leader understand their needs.[12] A leader who actively listens to their staff also promotes an environment where the staff feel safe to communicate.

As a leader, you need to show you are listening when staff bring concerns to you and be present in the conversation by responding, maintaining interest, and avoiding interruptions while they speak.[13] The more a leader encourages open communication and creates that environment, the better communication will be in the department between staff and leader.

Revisiting Donna

Donna, our manager from chapter 6, sent an email to the staff in a busy dermatology office. In her email, Donna informed the staff that one of the other providers would be out, so their office would be taking on extra patients. Donna was upset with her staff because she received multiple patient complaints. However, when Donna spoke with her staff, she found out that some had not read the email she sent, and others had just forgotten about it. So what could Donna have done differently?

As a leader, it was Donna's responsibility to make sure her staff understood the temporary change and that things went smoothly. Donna assumed that the staff had received the message by sending one email. When Donna heard of the plan to cover the patients from the other office, Donna should have gone to the office and had a meeting with the staff. She could have then followed up with an email. When meeting with the team, Donna could have allowed the staff to ask questions, and together they could have established the best plan to take on the extra patients without the staff being overwhelmed and the patients getting upset. Talking to the staff in person would have been an excellent opportunity for Donna to hear the concerns and consider moving a few additional staff members to the office.

If the change is happening in the future, it is up to the leader to remind the staff once the time approaches.

For example, if there were a week delay in the above situation, it is up to Donna to reach out to her staff to remind them what is happening and ask if they are still comfortable with the plan. By checking in with her team, Donna is following up to make sure that nothing has changed from their first meeting, but she can also provide any additional feedback she may have, like if she was able to get extra staff. Hopefully, Donna realizes that she cannot just send one email to her staff to communicate a coming change. Instead, she needs to take the time to explain the situation, get feedback and establish a plan with her staff.

CHAPTER 10

Strategies to Improve Leader Communication

Key Strategies

- ❖ Understand your audience.
- ❖ Use different methods to communicate important messages.
- ❖ Use different methods to communicate important messages.
    - o Email
    - o Text messages
    - o Posters in employee break rooms
- ❖ Understand what communication method works best for your team.
- ❖ Provide feedback.
- ❖ Provide a safe environment for communication.
- ❖ Actively listen when your team communicates.

Reflection Questions

- ❖ Of the presented strategies, in what areas do you feel you can improve?
- ❖ Do you understand how your team needs you to communicate?

CHAPTER 11

Strategies to Improve Leader & Employee Relationships

The single biggest way to impact an organization is to focus on leadership development. There is almost no limit to the potential of an organization that recruits good people, raises them up as leaders, and continually develops them.

—JOHN MAXWELL

Amy was feeling a little nervous but was super excited to be joining a new surgical services team as their director. She had finished her orientation and was looking forward to having a full day in her department.

Walking into the department, she noticed how some staff members headed in the other direction as others came to welcome her. Amy made sure to introduce herself and speak to each person. She listened to their stories about their history at the facility and tried to remember everything she could.

After settling in, Amy scheduled a department meeting for the following day. Amy walked through the department, meeting everyone she could throughout the day, and told them about the meeting the following day. The next day, Amy's staff were all present at the meeting.

After introducing herself again and giving a little of her history, she opened the floor up to the team. She asked to hear what they would like to see change within the department and what they felt worked well for the department.

After they finished talking, Amy went into her plan for the next thirty days. She told them her intentions to meet with each staff member and continue to get to know each of them and what they each bring to the department.

By the end of the meeting, Amy could identify some employees she felt were interested in high-quality relationships. Amy knew it would take time to identify the types of relationships all staff want, but she felt good about how things were starting.

CHAPTERS 8, 9, AND 10 COVERED DIFFERENT STRATEGIES leaders can use to improve employee perception of leader support, trust, and communication. These strategies include recognition, visibility, empowerment, being authentic, following through, understanding your audience, providing feedback, and finding what works best for your team. If leaders implement these strategies from chapters 8, 9, and 10, they will significantly impact their team and relationships.

Chapter 11 will discuss additional strategies that leaders can use to develop and improve the relationships between themselves and their staff by utilizing aspects of the LMX theory.

The relationships may be new if a leader is new to their role, or the relationships may already be intact but may need further development or repair.

Finally, we will revisit Tiffany, our new manager from chapter 7, who is unwelcoming to ideas and standoffish toward her staff.

Understanding the Relationship

As reviewed in chapter 7, LMX theory focuses on the relationship between leaders and employees and emphasizes the need for developing mature leadership relationships.[1]

One of the first steps to improving the interactions between leader and employee is understanding how relationships develop and the type of connections established. Relationships develop over time between a leader and their staff members, but it is essential to remember that the relationship development between a leader and employee involves both parties. It is not just a leader exerting influence over the employee but also the employee influencing a leader.[2] How leaders interact with their staff impacts the type of connections they will develop. And leaders may interact differently with staff members depending on how staff reacts to the interactions.

For example, like our manager, Tiffany, from chapter 7, if an employee is standoffish or unfriendly when a leader speaks with them, the leader may not try to develop that relationship any further.

Some employees will decide that having a higher-quality relationship does not benefit them, or some leaders will determine that an employee is not fit for a higher-quality relationship. It is the decision of the leader and team members as to how far one develops within the relationship. The importance of developing the right relationships occurs over time, and typically, they develop through various stages.[3] One of the most important things for a leader to do is to interact with the staff and understand, from those interactions, what types of relationships they see developing. As mentioned in chapter 7, the two types of relationships leaders may form with their employees are high quality and low quality. Both relationships are equally crucial to the success of the team.

Developing Relationships

Once a leader understands the importance of developing relationships, the next step is to *develop* them. The various stages of development show how relationships either become high quality or low quality through the continued interactions between leader and employee.

Relationship interactions between leader and employee begin at the basic level of exchanges during regular job tasks.[4] Also, during the initial phase, the leader attempts to discover the employee's talents and motivations, which helps the leader understand what type of relationship may develop.[5] As the leader and employee interact, both determine whether they are happy with one another and if the relationship is worth continuing.

For example, I have seen many cases where an employee will resign within the first few weeks on a job due to the job/leader not being what they thought. Or another reason may be a leader stating a new employee is not a fit, whether for the department or the organization.

For this reason, as stated in chapter 7, interviewing is *such* a critical step in the recruiting process. As a leader, you need to identify people with whom you can develop working relationships, and an interview also helps people see if they feel they will be a good fit with the leader. An employee must be a fit for the organization, leader, department, and team. I have seen many situations where a person may not fit with one leader but can develop a high-quality relationship with another.

During the phases of relationship development, the more interactions a leader has with their employees, the more the leader is building trust, showing support, and establishing communication. As the relationship grows, the employee decides whether they want to take on additional responsibilities, and the leader assesses the employee to see if they will be able to provide them with new challenges.[6] Additionally, several factors can influence the relationship between leader and follower, including the level of mutual trust, mutual loyalty, influence on one another, competence, and perceived equity of the relationship.[7] For these reasons, a leader and an employee must be authentic and intentional with their actions. Both parties need to determine whether they want the relationship to be at its strongest.

Improving Relationships

As leaders interact and develop their staff relationships, they can identify employees whom they are more compatible with and those who match the leader's leadership style.[8] These employees are looking to grow within the organization and are interested in taking on more responsibility. These employees are the ones who want more leader interaction and want to build those relationships.

As a leader, you need to identify your staff that want to grow and develop. Leaders need to take the time to talk to their employees and even ask them what their goals are. Show your staff you are engaged by listening, supporting, and helping them. By developing these high-quality relationships, the bond between the leader and employee exceeds the traditional work relationship and creates an effective way to accomplish the organization's goals.[9] But, remember, a leader will have both high- and low-quality relationships, so it is essential for a leader to identify and develop both types of relationships.

Leaders need to focus on both groups, whether they are low- or high-quality relationships and look for different ways to build trust and respect with all employees, thus building a stronger team.[10] Whether high or low, research shows that LMX relationships may affect job performance, satisfaction, commitment, role perceptions, and turnover intentions.[11] Therefore, a leader needs to understand the difference between the relationships and treat both fairly. Due to the correlations between relationships, we see why the LMX model is critical between leaders and their staff and why developing these relationships is essential.

Revisiting Tiffany

Our manager, Tiffany, from Rover Medical Center in chapter 7, is a newer leader in the hospital. Unfortunately, as her staff has tried to welcome her and develop relationships with her, Tiffany has been standoffish and not receptive to suggestions or open communication. Now, six months into her employment, Tiffany has a lot of work to do to improve and develop the relationships with her team. So what strategies can Tiffany take to connect with her team and identify the different relationships?

Tiffany needs to *want* to make the change with her team. She needs to take the time to interact with her staff. Instead of being standoffish, she needs to communicate and build trust with her employees. Though it has been six months, it would be beneficial for Tiffany to have a staff meeting and introduce herself and her plans for the department. Then she can go over the things she has observed over her first six months and what she would like to do to move forward. Tiffany could also identify those staff members that have brought ideas to her and follow up with them. Developing relationships takes time, but Tiffany must open the lines of communication.

Following the staff meeting, Tiffany should schedule individual meetings with her staff. During these meetings, she can ask them about any concerns they have or what they think is working well in the department. She can also ask them what changes they would like to see and their goals at the organization. These meetings will help Tiffany identify those employees who may be interested in high-quality relationships versus those who are not. It will be up to Tiffany to continue with intentional interactions with her staff while working on building trust and showing support for her staff. The more approachable and visible Tiffany makes herself, the more comfortable her staff will feel, and those relationships will develop over time.

CHAPTER 11

Strategies to Improve Leader
& Employee Relationships

Key Strategies

- ❖ Understand the different relationships.

- ❖ Identify which type of relationship employees want.

- ❖ Work on developing relationships with staff.

- ❖ Be intentional and interact with staff to improve relationships.

- ❖ Focus on both high- and low-quality relationships.

Reflection Questions

- ❖ Are you able to identify the different relationships you have with your team?

- ❖ Are there relationships that you need to improve?

Organizational Implications of Improved Leader Support

There are no secrets to success. It is the result of preparation, hard work, and learning from failure.

—COLIN POWELL

Every year, we had a company picnic, but they stopped that. They care about money; they do not care about the employees. The company does not appreciate what we do. Does the organization even realize what we are dealing with? I am retiring after thirty years, and no one from the administration even came to my retirement party at work. I see my leader every day, but I have never met anyone from administration.

These comments are all things employees say when they feel unsupported or disconnected from the organization.

WHEN LEADERS STRIVE TO IMPROVE THEMSELVES AND THEIR relationships with employees, what does that mean for the organization? First, the previous chapters looked at employee perceptions of leader support, trust, communication, and leader-employee relationships. Next, I presented strategies to assist leaders in improving employee perceptions. Then, looking further in depth, what implications will improved employee perceptions in these areas have on the organization? Additionally, what does an organization gain by having leaders who truly understand what their employees need?

The previous chapters show that better employee perception of their leader's support, trust, and communication will result in higher-quality relationships with their leader. An employee chooses how much effort they want to give to an organization, which determines the level of relationship they build with their leader.

This chapter will examine how improving and maintaining a positive leader-employee relationship will affect the organization and why organizations should promote an LMX approach.

Next, we will look at the organization's ability to show support by improving trust and communication and encouraging positive, high-quality relationships.

LMX Organizational Implications

Increased employee retention and job satisfaction are two of the main benefits of increased leader support and increased morale, which employees feel throughout the organization. Research has shown that higher-quality relationships have positive outcomes for all aspects of an organization due to the positive characteristics and behaviors influencing the leader and employee relationship.[1] The better the relationship between a leader and their employee, the more beneficial it is to an organization. Organizations can base the quality of this relationship on the exchange of resources, which could influence employees' perceptions of trust and obligation toward their leaders.[2] Higher-quality LMX relationships are related to better job performance, higher overall satisfaction, more commitment, better communication, less role conflict, more role clarity, the competence of leaders and followers, and less intention to quit.[3] By managing high-quality relationships, leaders affect critical organizational outcomes because the relationships are critical factors for socialization and reducing employee stress and turnover.[4]

As discussed in previous chapters, employees who feel supported by their leaders are beyond satisfied, work better within their team, and are less likely to leave. In addition, the more satisfied employees are, the less likely they are to look for jobs elsewhere, even when they are working short-staffed or are feeling burned out.

In times of high stress, morale across an organization may dwindle. Stressors can include increased gas prices, personal family issues, higher-acuity patients, or increased employee openings. Therefore, leaders must maintain a pulse on their department and team members.

For example, when a leader hears talk of unhappiness or discouragement among their staff due to the rising cost of housing, food, and gas prices, it may be worth a conversation with administration and human resources about looking at a possible cost of living increase. In this case, it is up to the organization to decide the next course of action, but at least the leader heard the needs of their staff and presented them to the next level of leadership.

In many organizations, the front-line leaders are more aware of employees' level of satisfaction and morale than upper management. Thus, leaders need to communicate with upper management, keeping them from being surprised if something arises.

By encouraging leader and employee relationships, organizations have the potential for opportunities to gain valuable insight into different organizational functions across the different organizational levels.[5] Whether they be between a leader and their employees or between leaders, relationships within an organization are critical.

For example, LMX encourages leadership relationships among peers, teammates, and across organizational levels to build stronger bonds throughout the organization.[6] The stronger bond throughout the organization helps leaders identify and respond to any concerns. Additionally, LMX reduces job insecurity, stress, and emotional exhaustion, resulting in decreased turnover.[7] Also, by examining the relationships among leaders, an organization should be able to see those leaders who develop relationships with their staff and those who focus on other areas.

For example, if a leader has more low-quality relationships, the organization could see low productivity and job satisfaction.[8] So suppose an organization observes areas of lower morale and employee satisfaction. In that case, they may need to investigate the type of relationship leaders have with their employees and what actions they should take.

Organizational Actions

What can organizations do to show they support their workforce? Businesses can show employees they care in many different ways.

For example, with the pandemic came an increased need for mental health benefits. As a result, many organizations added or enhanced the mental health benefits they offer to employees. In addition, many organizations revisited their entire benefits program to ensure that what they offer meets the needs and demands of their employees. Even such things as the fringe benefits, like tuition reimbursement, on-site childcare, paid time off, etc., have all been enhanced or added. Employers also encourage their employees to go back to school, so I know certain healthcare providers are even offering full tuition assistance to further employee education. By improving their benefits, organizations show that they care about their employees' well-being and goals to better themselves.

Another area that employees have struggled with is their work-life balance and schedules. Many employers had to examine the opportunity for their employees to work from home. If leaders hear that an employee is struggling to make things work due to a scheduling conflict or something else, if the organization can make reasonable accommodations to a schedule, they should.

Many organizations have worked with their employees to set up remote workstations or flexible schedules.

For example, I know many organizations where, when employees turned in their resignation due to the cost of childcare or not finding childcare, the organizations were able to retain those employees by offering a more flexible schedule or the opportunity to work remotely.

Companywide activities are another excellent way for organizations to show their support and appreciation for their employees. Along with leaders recognizing their employees, organizations need to take part in recognizing and appreciating employees. Whether it be companywide picnics, service and recognition events, or small tokens of appreciation, these events are all ways an organization can do something thoughtful for their staff.

For example, service awards are an excellent way for an organization to make a big deal about those employees who hit certain employment milestones. Again, employees do not need something extravagant, but do they need to know that their employer appreciates everything they do and recognizes their hard work.

As leaders, we understand that we cannot make everyone happy. Employees may (and will) be disgruntled for a variety of reasons, and concerns and situations will arise that recognition or a picnic will not fix. However, organizations can train and encourage their leaders to develop better relationships with their staff that benefits everyone. Implementing LMX tends to improve employees' feelings of organizational support, burnout, and communication, helping to improve overall commitment and satisfaction, resulting in a decline in turnover.

If a leader is aware and in touch with their team, they will hear the concerns, whether it be rising gas prices or higher competitor pay. It is up to the organization to help leaders understand what to do when they hear different concerns happening within the company. Organizations need to provide the vision and resources to help leaders be successful with their employees and ensure that all employees, including leaders, feel supported. If an organization wants to have a committed workforce, research has shown that organizations should provide a supportive work environment that will increase employees' level of commitment and reduce employees' intentions to quit.[9]

Something else that an organization can do is look at turnover and see if any trends are showing.

For example, if many employees leave within their first ninety days or six months, maybe HR needs to revamp new hires' onboarding and orientation process.

Many different situations may affect an employee, so leaders and organizations must be connected to their workforce. No matter the employee's role, there are positive implications when an employee feels supported by their leader and organization.

CHAPTER 12

Organizational Implications of Improved Leader Support

Key Strategies

- ❖ Organizations should encourage leader and employee relationships.

- ❖ Revisit and enhance employee benefits, including mental health benefits.

- ❖ Be flexible where you are able.

- ❖ Bring back organization-wide activities to show appreciation.

Reflection Questions

- ❖ Does your organization encourage and support leader and employee relationships?

- ❖ Do you feel supported by your organization? If not, what should change?

CHAPTER 13

Tying it All Together

Successful organizations understand the importance of implementation, not just strategy, and, moreover, recognize the crucial role of their people in this process.

—JEFFREY PFEFFER

THROUGHOUT THIS GUIDE, I PROVIDED DIFFERENT EXAMPLES and scenarios that healthcare leaders may face throughout their day. I hope that through these scenarios, you have been able to see how critical it is for leaders to support their employees in different ways. Support can encompass many different things, and a leader needs to ensure they understand and support what their employees need.

Being a leader comes with many responsibilities. In addition, you have organizational demands like productivity, financial goals, and high patient satisfaction scores. Finally, as a leader, it is beneficial to you to have a successful team, making you a successful leader. The more you support your team in their work, the more committed they are to you, the department, and the organization. To be supportive, though, a leader needs to ensure they communicate and create an environment of trust while building and developing high-quality relationships with their staff. A leader who develops these qualities with their team will be able to retain employees within the organization.

At the beginning of the guide, I discussed how critical it is for a leader to understand their employees' challenges. Leaders can better focus their attention on those areas by understanding these challenges. In addition, the more a leader understands their team, the more support and attention the leader can give. A leader giving more support and attention thus leads to increased trust, improved communication, and better overall relationships with employees.

If an organization has leaders who create environments where employees feel safe and supported, it needs to ensure it is doing the same things for its leaders. No matter their level, every employee needs to feel that their leader supports them and that they can trust their leader. There also needs to be an environment of open communication and some type of relationship between leader and employee. The more an organization understands the needs of its workforce, the more it can address concerns and build a stronger and more satisfied team. With a happy and robust team, the organization will be able to meet its organizational goals and ensure it continues to be successful. Through all the changes the healthcare industry faces, only those organizations that can provide their leaders and employees with support will be able to retain their high-quality workers.

My purpose for this guide was to help healthcare leaders understand that they will face many challenges throughout their careers. It is essential to understand that to solve some of those significant challenges, leaders will need to understand what their employees need at that time. As I discussed in the different chapters, leaders can fix many challenges with simple solutions.

It is not always easy for leaders to slow down and listen to what their employees need, but I hope this guide shows you the positive implications of leaders taking the extra time to listen and understand. It is essential to understand that leaders will always face challenges, and not all of them will have a simple fix. But if a leader can identify the areas in which they can improve, hopefully, some of those significant challenges will not seem so bad. I also hope that the key points or strategies and the reflection questions help you reflect on your organization and leadership style.

As you have read the chapters, there may be certain areas where you feel you are meeting your employees' needs, but there may be others where you aren't. I have accomplished my goal if this guide helped you recognize areas you or your organization may need to improve. The more we can do as leaders to be more self-aware and aware of the needs of our team, the better and more successful we will be. After all, leadership is about leading others to be successful, and we can only do that if we take the time to understand how we can accomplish success together.

Appendix

Now that you have read different scenarios and strategies about different aspects of leader and organizational support, it is time to assess your organization. To assess your organization, here are the critical strategies presented in each chapter and the follow-up questions. Reviewing these strategies and questions as a leadership team will allow leaders to assess their strengths and weaknesses as a leader. Also, as a team, leaders will better understand where the organization is currently and where it needs to head in the future to meet the needs of the employees. These discussions may show that the organization needs to do more to assess the status of the employees. There are a lot of different resources out there that can be used, like performing stay interviews or specific assessments on the level of perceived trust, communication, etc.

Key Points and Strategies Presented

- All employees need to feel supported, no matter their level.
- Support comes in many different forms and means different things to different people.
- Relationships are critical between a leader and employee within an organization.
- Organizations face several different challenges.

- Leaders need to focus on the challenges they can make the most impact on, like communication and retention.

- Employees want different things; the goal is to identify their needs.

- Identify the top performers within your team and understand their goals within the organization.

- Be flexible where you can.

- Support is essential for the retention of employees.

- Show employees you care by acknowledging their concerns.

- Support is the responsibility of the whole organization, not just front-line leaders.

- An employee's perception of their leader affects the level of trust the employee perceives.

- Employees trust their organizations to keep them safe, pay them for work performed, and have the employee's best interests in mind.

- Communication is essential for any organization to be successful.

- Communication provides direction toward the overall organizational goals and expectations.

- Communication should occur in different ways to ensure employees receive the intended message.

- Mutual trust, loyalty, and influence determine the level of the relationship.

- Leaders should have both high-quality and low-quality relationships.

- Recognize your employees in a variety of ways.
- Take the time to address your employee's concerns.
- Be visible!
- Empower and inspire your team!
- Do not make excuses for employees' bad behavior.
- Be present and authentic.
- Follow through with things brought to your attention.
- Ask and encourage questions.
- Help your staff members grow!
- Do not allow an environment of gossip.
- Understand your audience.
- Use different methods to communicate important messages.
  - Email
  - Text messages
  - Posters in employee break rooms
- Understand what communication method works best for your team.
- Provide feedback.
- Provide a safe environment for communication.
- Actively listen when your team communicates.
- Understand the different relationships.
- Identify which type of relationship employees want.
- Work on developing relationships with staff.
- Be intentional and interact with staff to improve relationships.

- Organizations should encourage leader and employee relationships.
- Revisit and enhance employee benefits, including mental health benefits.
- Be flexible where you are able.
- Bring back organization-wide activities to show appreciation.

Key Questions to Discuss with Your Leaders

- What are some current struggles that you are seeing within your organization?
- Do you see that struggles throughout the organization are more concentrated in certain areas?
- What do you think your employees want?
- Do you think your employees want a deeper connection with you as their leader?
- What do you think your employees want from your organization that they are not getting now?
- Do you check in with your staff daily?
- When things seem overwhelming in your department, do you jump in to help?
- Does your organization schedule time when there are no meetings so that leaders can do the things needed within their departments?
- How do you handle the situation when an employee brings a concern to you?
- Does your team feel that if they bring a concern to you, they can trust you to follow up on it?

- How do you communicate with your team?
- Do you only use one mode of communication, or do you use several so that you know the message is received?
- How does your organization communicate essential things?
- What type of relationships do you have with your employees?
- Can you identify your employees with whom you could have high-quality relationships? And those that you could have low-quality relationships?
- Does your organization value the different relationships with employees?
- Of the strategies presented, which could you implement with your staff to provide leader support?
- Do you find yourself excusing bad behavior instead of confronting the issue?
- Of the presented strategies, in what areas do you feel you can improve?
- Would your team say that you lead by example?
- Do you understand how your team needs you to communicate?
- Are you able to identify the different relationships you have with your team?
- Are there relationships that you need to improve?
- Does your organization encourage and support leader and employee relationships?
- Do you feel supported by your organization? If not, what should change?

Notes

Chapter 1: Introduction and Personal Story

[1] Levine, D., "U.S. Faces Crisis of Burned-Out Health Care Workers," U.S. News & World Report, November 15, 2021, https://www.usnews.com/news/health-news/articles/2021-11-15/us-faces-crisis-of-burned-out-health-care-workers.

[2] "Supportive Leadership," Resources, Corporate Finance Institute, 2015, https://corporatefinanceinstitute.com/resources/careers/soft-skills/supportive-leadership/.

[3] Jung, J, & Kim, Y, "Causes of Newspaper Firm Employee Burnout in Korea and its Impact on Organizational Commitment and Turnover Intention," *The International Journal of Human Resource Management* 23, no. 17 (2012): 3,636–3,651.

[4] Graen, G, & Uhl-Bien, M, "The Transformation of Professionals into Self-Managing and Partially Self-Designing Contributions,," *Journal of Management Systems* 3, no. 3 (1991): 25–39.

Chapter 2: Current Challenges

[1] Holloran, K, Repucci, S, & Sonola, O., "Not-for Profit Healthcare Staffing Shortage has Long-Term Effects,," Fitch Wire, October 27, 2021, https://www.fitchratings.com/research/us-public-finance/not-for-profit-healthcare-staffing-shortage-has-long-term-effects-27-10-2021.

[2] Korcok, M., "'Perfect Storm' Brewing in U.S. Because of Nursing Shortage: CMAJ," *Canadian Medical Association Journal* 167, no. 10 (Nov 12, 2002): 1,159. Available at https://www.proquest.com/scholarly-journals/perfect-storm-brewing-us-because-nursing-shortage/docview/204956602/se-2.

[3] Maurer, R., "Great expectations,," *HR Magazine*, Winter 2021: 32–39.

Notes

[4] Holloran, K., Repucci, S., & Sonola, O., "Not-for Profit Healthcare Staffing Shortage has Long-Term Effects," Fitch Wire, October 27, 2021, https://www.fitchratings.com/research/us-public-finance/not-for-profit-healthcare-staffing-shortage-has-long-term-effects-27-10-2021.

[5] Gimbel, M. & Sinclair, T., "Larger Skills Gap in Healthcare than in Overall Economy," Indeed Hiring Lab, March 20, 2019, https://www.hiringlab.org/2019/03/20/healthcare-skills-gap/.

[6] Gooch, K., "6 Predictions for the Future Healthcare Workforce," December 19, 2021, https://www.beckershospitalreview.com/workforce/6-predictions-for-the-future-healthcare-workforcehtml.

[7] Holloran, K., Repucci, S., & Sonola, O., "Not-for Profit Healthcare Staffing Shortage has Long-Term Effects," Fitch Wire, October 27, 2021, https://www.fitchratings.com/research/us-public-finance/not-for-profit-healthcare-staffing-shortage-has-long-term-effects-27-10-2021.

[8] Liu, J.X., Goryakin, Y., Maeda, A., "Global Health Workforce Labor Market Projections for 2030," *Human Resource Health* 15, no. 11 (2017), https://doi.org/10.1186/s12960-017-0187-2.

[9] "Student Enrollment Surged in U.S. Schools of Nursing in 2020 Despite Challenges Presented by the Pandemic," American Association of Colleges of Nursing, April 01, 2021, Student Enrollment Surged in U.S. Schools of Nursing in 2020 Despite Challenges Presented by the Pandemic (aacnnursing.org).

[10] Davies, R., "7 Key Employee Retention Strategies for Your Small Business," Blueprint, November 30, 2020, A Beginner's Guide to Employee Retention in 2021 | The Blueprint (fool.com).

[11] Davies, R., "7 Key Employee Retention Strategies for Your Small Business," Blueprint, November 30, 2020, A Beginner's Guide to Employee Retention in 2021 | The Blueprint (fool.com).

[12] Warrick, D., & Gardner, D., "Leaders build cultures: Action steps for leaders to build successful organizational cultures," *Journal of Leadership, Accountability and Ethics* 18, no. 1 (2021): 36–52 https://doi.org/10.33423/jlae.v18i1.4002.

[13] Levi, D., "Group Dynamics for Teams," 5th ed, (Thousand Oaks, CA: Sage Publications, 2017): n.p.

[14] "Everything you Need to Know about Nurse Burnout," The Well-Being Index, https://www.mywellbeingindex.org/nurse-burnout.

[15] Tuma, R., "Burnout may be Costing your Institution Millions Each Year," Medscape, October 17, 2017, https://www.medscape.com/viewarticle/887195.

[16] "Everything you Need to Know about Nurse Burnout," The Well-Being Index, https://www.mywellbeingindex.org/nurse-burnout.

[17] "Everything you Need to Know about Nurse Burnout," The Well-Being Index, https://www.mywellbeingindex.org/nurse-burnout.

[18] Kuepers, J., "Manager Burnout: 16 Harrowing Statistics from 2021," HR Morning, December 20, 2021, https://www.hrmorning.com/articles/manager-burnout.

[19] Case, T., "Managing stress: Company leaders face pressure, burnout just as employees do," Digiday, July 12, 2021, https://digiday.com/marketing/managing-stress-company-leaders-face-pressure-burnout-just-as-employees-do/.

[20] Place, A., "How Managers can Protect Themselves from Burnout," Employee Benefits Network, March 11, 2021, https://www.benefitnews.com/news/how-managers-can-protect-themselves-from-burnout.

[21] Kuepers, J., "Manager Burnout: 16 Harrowing Statistics from 2021," HR Morning, December 20, 2021, https://www.hrmorning.com/articles/manager-burnout.

[22] Mitra, A., Jenkins, G., & Gupta, N., "A Meta-Analytic Review of the Relationship Between Absence and Turnover," *Journal of*

Applied Psychology 77, no 6 (1992): 879–889. https://doi.org/10 .1037/0021-9010.77.6.879.

[23] Eddy, N., "Staffing Shortages Ramp up Recruitment Pressure on Hospitals," *Healthcare Finance*, October 7, 2021, https:// www.healthcarefinancenews.com/news/staffing-shortages-ramp -recruitment-pressure-hospitals.

Chapter 3: What Do Employees Want

[1] McGovern, M., "Retain Employees Now: 5 Ways to Stop the Exodus," HR Morning, August 17, 2021, https://www .hrmorning.com/articles/retan-employees-2/.

[2] Ahmetoglu, G., Nefyodova, V., Chamorro-Premuziv, T., & Codreanu, S., "What Leads Entrepreneurial Employees to Want to Quit, or Stay in, Their Job? Exploring Two Conflicting Mechanisms," *Applied Psychology* 70, no. 2 (2021): 738–758, https://doi.org/10.1111/apps.12250.

[3] Aiello, F., Grover, R., Andrews, B., Herszkopf, J., "Knowing What Your Employees Want in the Workplace: A Source of Competitive Advantage," *Competition Forum* 3, no. 2 (2005): 261–270.

[4] McGovern, M., "Retain Employees Now: 5 Ways to Stop the Exodus," HR Morning, August 17, 2021, https://www .hrmorning.com/articles/retan-employees-2/.

[5] McGovern, M., "Retain Employees Now: 5 Ways to Stop the Exodus," HR Morning, August 17, 2021, https://www .hrmorning.com/articles/retan-employees-2/.

[6] McGovern, M., "Retain Employees Now: 5 Ways to Stop the Exodus," HR Morning, August 17, 2021, https://www .hrmorning.com/articles/retan-employees-2/.

[7] McGovern, M., "8 Ways to Improve the Employee Experience in 2022," HR Morning, December 14, 2021, https://www .hrmorning.com/articles/employee-experience-2022.

[8] McGovern, M., "Retain Employees Now: 5 Ways to Stop the Exodus," HR Morning, August 17, 2021, https://www.hrmorning.com/articles/retan-employees-2/.

[9] Pieniazek, J., "Getting Ahead—Americans Share About Raises & Promotions," LiveCareer, July 21, 2021, Getting Ahead—Americans Share About Raises & Promotions | LiveCareer.

[10] Cheng, Z., Liu, W., Zhou, K, Che, Y., & Han, Y., "Promoting Employees' Pro-Environmental Behavior Through Empowering Leadership: The Toles of Psychological Ownership, Empowerment Role Identity, and Environmental Self-Identity," *Business Ethics, the Environment & Responsibility* 30, no. 4 (2021): 604–618, https://doi.org/10.1111/beer.12366.

[11] Bayuk, J., "Should Employers Prioritize Internal Promotions? Companies with High Rates of Internal Hires Experience Greater Retention," *HR Magazine*, Winter 2021: 30–31.

[12] Pieniazek, J., "Getting Ahead—Americans Share About Raises & Promotions," LiveCareer, July 21, 2021, Getting Ahead—Americans Share About Raises & Promotions | LiveCareer.

[13] Maurer, R., "Great Expectations," *HR Magazine*, Winter 2021: 32–39.

[14] McGovern, M., "8 Ways to Improve the Employee Experience in 2022," HR Morning, December 14, 2021, 8 ways to improve the employee experience in 2022 | HR Morning.

[15] Grensing-Pohal, L., "Recruiting in a Pandemic," *HR Magazine*, Spring 2021: 51–56.

[16] Meinecke, A. & Kauffeld, S., "Engaging the Hearts and Minds of Followers: Leader Empathy and Language Style Matching During Appraisal Interviews," *Journal of Business & Psychology* 34 (2019): 485–501, https://doi.org/10.1007/s10869-018-9554-9.

[17] Agovino, T., "What you Need to Succeed," *HR Magazine*, Winter 2021: 48–53.

[18] Meinecke, A. & Kauffeld, S., "Engaging the Hearts and Minds of Followers: Leader Empathy and Language Style Matching During Appraisal Interviews," *Journal of Business & Psychology* 34 (2019): 485–501, https://doi.org/10.1007/s10869-018-9554-9.

[19] McGovern, M., "8 Ways to Improve the Employee Experience in 2022," HR Morning, December 14, 2021, 8 ways to improve the employee experience in 2022 | HR Morning.

Chapter 4: Leader Support

[1] Li, S., Jia, R., Seufert, J., QNG, x., & Luo, J. (2020), "Ambidextrous Leadership and Radical Innovative Capability: The Moderating Role of Leader Support," *Creativity and Innovation Management* 29, no. 4: 621–633, https://doi.org/10.1111/caim.12402.

[2] Locke, E., "The nature and consequences of job satisfaction," in M. Dunnette (ed.), *Handbook of Industrial and Organizational Psychology* (Chicago: Rand McNally, 1976),1,297–1,349.

[3] Carmeli, A., & Weisberg, J., "Exploring turnover intentions among three professional groups of employees," *Human Resource Development International* 9, no. 2 (2006): 191–206, https://doi.org/10.1080/13678860600616305.

[4] Fritzsche, B., & Parrish, T., "Theories and Research on Job Satisfaction," in S. D. Brown & R. W. Lent (eds.) *Career Development and Counseling: Putting Theory and Research to Work* (New York: Wiley & Sons, *2005),* 180–202.

[5] Baer, M. & Oldham, G., "The Curvilinear Relation Between Experienced Creative Time Pressure and Creativity: Moderating Effects of Openness to Experience and Support for Creativity," *Journal of Applied Psychology* 91, no. 4 (2006): 963–970, https://doi.org/10.1037/0021-9010.91.4.963.

[6] Cho, S., Johanson, M., & Guchait, P., "Employees Intent to Leave: A Comparison of Determinants of Intent to Leave Versus Intent

to Stay," *International Journal of Hospitality Management* 28 (2009): 374–381, https://doi.org/10.1016/j.ijhm.2008.10.007.

[7] "Supportive Leadership: A Leadership Style that Supports an Employee until the Tasks Completion," CFI, accessed January 15, 2022, https://corporatefinanceinstitute.com/resources/careers /soft-skills/supportive-leadership/.

[8] Pelenk, S., "The Mediation Effect of Leader Support in the Effect of Organizational Commitment on Job Satisfaction: A Research in the Turkish Textile Business," *International Journal of Organizational Business* 9 (2020): 227–242, https://doi.org/10 .33844/ijol.2020.60508.

[9] Bakker, A.B., Demerouti, E., & Dollard, M.F., "How Job Demands Affect Partners' Experience of Exhaustion: Integrating Work-family Conflict and Crossover Theory," *Journal of Applied Psychology* 93 (2008): 901–911.

[10] Li, S., Jia, R., Seufert, J., QNG, x., & Luo, J., "Ambidextrous Leadership and Radical Innovative Capability: The Moderating Role of Leader Support," *Creativity and Innovation Management* 29, no. 4 (2020): 621–633, https://doi.org/10.1111/caim.12402.

[11] Trepanier, S., Henderson, R., & Wagbray, A., "A Health Care System's Approach to Support Nursing Leaders in Mitigating Burnout Amid a COVID-19 World Pandemic," *Nursing Administration Quarterly* 1, no. 46 (2022): 52–59, https://doi.org /10.1097/NAQ.0000000000000507

[12] Dawley, D.D., Andrews, M.C., & Bucklew, N.S., "Mentoring, Supervisor Support, and Perceived Organizational Support: What Matters Most?" *Leadership & Organization Development Journal* 29, no. 3 (2008): 235–247, https://doi.org/10.1108 /01437730810861290.

[13] Choi, W., Kanf, S., & Choi, S., "Innovative Behavior in the Workplace: An Empirical Study of Moderated Mediation Model of Self-Efficacy, Perceived Organizational Support, and Leader-

Member Exchange," *Behavioral Sciences* 11, no. 182 (2021): 1–17.

[14] Trepanier, S., Henderson, R., & Wagbray, A., "A Health Care System's Approach to Support Nursing Leaders in Mitigating Burnout Amid a COVID-19 World Pandemic," *Nursing Administration Quarterly* 1, no 46 (2022): 52–59, https://doi.org/10.1097/NAQ.0000000000000507.

Chapter 5: Leader Trust

[1] Kim, S., "Enticing High Performers to Stay and Share their Knowledge: The Importance of Trust in Leader," *Human Resource Management* 58, no. 4 (2019): 341–351, https://doi.org/10.1002/hrm.21955.

[2] Burke, C., Sims, D., Lazzara, E., & Sal, E., "Trust in Leadership: A Multi-Level Review and Integration," *The Leadership Quarterly* 18 (2007): 606–632, https://doi.org/10.1016/j.leaqua.2007.09.006.

[3] Mayer, R., Davis, J., Shoorman, F., "An Integrative Model of Organizational Trust," *Academy of Management Review* 20 (1995): 709–734.

[4] Nyhan, R., "Changing the Paradigm: Trust and its Role in Public Sector Organizations," *The American Review of Public Administration* 30 (2000): 87–109, https://doi.org/c34kbx.

[5] Burke, C., Sims, D., Lazzara, E., & Sal, E., "Trust in Leadership: A Multi-Level Review and Integration," *The Leadership Quarterly* 18 (2007): 606–632, https://doi.org/10.1016/j.leaqua.2007.09.006.

[6] Burke, C., Sims, D., Lazzara, E., & Sal, E., "Trust in Leadership: A Multi-Level Review and Integration," *The Leadership Quarterly* 18 (2007): 606–632, https://doi.org/10.1016/j.leaqua.2007.09.006.

[7] Schoormann, F., Mayer, R., & Davis, J., "An Integrative Model of Organizational Trust: Past, Present and Future," *Academy of Management Review* 32 (2007): 344–354, https://doi.org/bwcntq.

[8] Kim, S., "Enticing High Performers to Stay and Share their Knowledge: The Importance of Trust in Leader," *Human Resource Management* 58, no. 4 (2019): 341–351, https://doi.org /10.1002/hrm.21955.

[9] Phong, L., Hui, L., & Son, T., "How Leadership and Trust in Leaders Foster Employees' Behavior Towards Knowledge Sharing," *Social Behavior and Personality* 46, no. 5 (2018): 705–720, https://doi.org/10.2224/sbp.6711.

[10] Zand, D., "Trust and Managerial Problem-Solving," *Administrative Science Quarterly* 17, no. 2 (1972): 229–239, https://doi.org/10 .2307/2393957.

[11] Burke, C., Sims, D., Lazzara, E., & Sal, E., "Trust in Leadership: A Multi-Level Review and Integration," *The Leadership Quarterly* 18 (2007): 606–632, https://doi.org/10.1016/j.leaqua.2007.09 .006.

[12] Burke, C., Sims, D., Lazzara, E., & Sal, E., "Trust in Leadership: A Multi-Level Review and Integration," *The Leadership Quarterly* 18 (2007): 606–632, https://doi.org/10.1016/j.leaqua.2007.09 .006.

[13] Dirks, K., "Trust in Leadership and Team Performance: Evidence from NCAA Basketball," *Journal of Applied Psychology* 65, no. 6 (2000): 1,004–1,012, https://doi.org/10.1037/0021-9010.85 .6.1004.

[14] Davis, J., Shoorman, F., Mayer, R., & Tan, H., "The Trusted General Manager and Business Unit Performance: Empirical Evidence of a Competitive Advantage," *Strategic Management Journal* 21, no. 5 (2000): 563–579, https://doi.org/10.1002 /(SICI)1097-0266(200005)21:5<563::AID-SMJ99>3.0.CO;2-0.

[15] Kim, S., "Enticing High Performers to Stay and Share their Knowledge: The Importance of Trust in Leader," *Human Resource Management* 58, no. 4 (2019): 341–351, https://doi.org/10.1002/hrm.21955.

[16] Mayer, R., & Gavin, M., "Trust in Management and Performance: Who Minds the Shop while the Employees Watch the Boss?" *Academy of Management Journal* 48, no. 5 (2005): 874–888, https://doi.org/10.5465/amj.2005.18803928.

[17] Vogus, T. & Sutcliffe, K., "The Impact of Safety Organizing Trusted Leadership, and Care Pathways on Reported Medication Errors in Hospital Nursing Units," *Medical Care* 45, no. 10 (2007): 997–1002, https://doi.org/10.1097/mlr.0bo13e318053674f.

[18] Burke, C., Sims, D., Lazzara, E., & Sal, E., "Trust in Leadership: A Multi-Level Review and Integration," *The Leadership Quarterly* 18 (2007): 606–632, https://doi.org/10.1016/j.leaqua.2007.09.006.

Chapter 6: Leader Communication

[1] Levi, D., "Group Dynamics for Teams," 5th ed. (Thousand Oaks, CA: Sage Publications, 2017), n.p.

[2] Parker, S.K., Axtell, C.M., & Turner, N., "Designing a Safer Workplace: Importance of Job Autonomy, Communication Quality, and Supportive Supervisors," *Journal of Occupational Health Psychology* 6, no. 3 (2001): 211–228, https://doi.org/10.1037/1076-8998.6.3.211.

[3] Veberg, R.M., Bosch-Sijtsema, P., & Vartiainen, M., "Getting it Done: Critical Success Factors for Project Managers in Virtual Work Settings," *International Journal of Project Management* 31 (2013): 68–79, https://doi:10.1016/j.ijproman.2012.04.005.

[4] Momeny, L., & Gourgues, M., "Communication that Develops Teams: Healthy Ministry Team Dynamics as a Function of Consistent Leader Communication of Emotional Intelligence," *Christian Education Journal: Research on Educational*

Ministry 17, no. 2 (2020): 283–297, https://doi:10.1177
/0739891319876288.

[5] Veberg, R.M., Bosch-Sijtsema, P., & Vartiainen, M., "Getting it
Done: Critical Success Factors for Project Managers in Virtual
Work Settings," *International Journal of Project Management* 31
(2013): 68–79, https://doi:10.1016/j.ijproman.2012.04.005.

[6] DeSanctis, G. & Monge, P., "Communication Processes for Virtual
Organizations," *Journal of Computer-Mediated Communication* 3,
no.4 (1998): 693–703, https://doi:10.1111/j.1083-6101.1998
.tb00083.x.

[7] Little, J., "Learning Through "Huddles" for Health Care Leaders:
Why Do Some Work Teams Learn as a Result of Huddles and
Others Do Not?," *The Health Care Manager* 33, no. 4 (2014):
335–341, https://doi:10.1097/HCM.0000000000000034.

[8] Ford, R., Piccolo, R., & Ford, L., "Strategies for Building Effective
Virtual Teams: Trust is Essential," *Business Horizons* 60 (2016):
25–34.

[9] Ceylan, C., & Yavas, H., "What Affects Employee Motivation at IT
Projects in Turkey? The Impact of Leader Communication, Wage
Satisfaction, and Job Opportunities at IT Projects Employee's,"
Balıkesir Üniversitesi Sosyal Bilimler Enstitüsü Dergisi 23, no. 44
(2020): 1,041–1,067.

[10] Merrim, K., Schmidt, S., & Dunlap-Hinkler, D., "Profiling
Virtual Employees: The Impact of Managing Virtually," *Journal
of Leadership & Organizational Studies* 14, no. 1 (2007): 6–15,
https://doi.org/10.1177/1071791907304244.

[11] Henderson, L, Stackman, R., & Lindekilde, R., "The Centrality
of Communication Norm Alignment, Role Clarity, and Trust
in Global Project Teams," *International Journal of Project
Management* 34 (2016): 1,717–1,194.

[12] Merrim, K., Schmidt, S., & Dunlap-Hinkler, D., "Profiling
Virtual Employees: The Impact of Managing Virtually," *Journal*

of Leadership & Organizational Studies 14, no. 1 (2007): 6–15, https://doi.org/10.1177/1071791907304244.

[13] Irawati, R., Susita, D., & Eryanto, H., "The Influence of Training and Organizational Communication on Job Loyalty with Job Satisfaction as an Intervening Variable," *Economics & Management* 4, no. 94 (2021): 99–108, https://doi.org/10.33146 /2307-9878-2021-4(94)-99-108.

[14] Little, J., "Learning Through 'Huddles' for Health Care Leaders: Why Do Some Work Teams Learn as a Result of Huddles and Others Do Not?," *The Health Care Manager* 33, no. 4 (2014): 335–341, https://doi.org/10.1097/HCM.0000000000000034.

[15] Irawati, R., Susita, D., & Eryanto, H., "The Influence of Training and Organizational Communication on Job Loyalty with Job Satisfaction as an Intervening Variable," *Economics & Management* 4, no. 94 (2021): 99–108, https://doi.org/10.33146 /2307-9878-2021-4(94)-99-108.

[16] Anders, R., "Practical Tips for Effective Communication," *Nursing Management* 52, no.6 (2021): 10–13, https://doi.org/10.1097/01 .NUMA.0000752812.54583.D6.

Chapter 7: Leader & Employee Relations

[1] Graen, G., & Uhl-Bien, M., "Relationship-Based Approach to Leadership: Development of Leader-Member Exchange (LMX) Theory of Leadership Over 25 Years: Applying a Multi-Level Multi-Domain Perspective," *The Leadership Quarterly* 6, no. 2 (1995): 219–247, https://doi.org/10.1016/1048-9843(95)90036 -5.

[2] Hollander, E., *Leadership Dynamics: A Practical Guide to Effective Relationships*, 6th ed. (New York: Free Press 1978), n.p.

[3] Graen, G., & Uhl-Bien, M., "The Transformation of Professionals into Self-Managing and Partially Self-Designing Contributions," *Journal of Management Systems* 3, no. 3 (1991): 25–39.

[4] Graen, G., "Role-Making Processes of Leadership Development," in M. D. Dunnette (ed.) *Handbook of Industrial and Organizational Psychology* (Chicago: Rand McNally, 1976), 1,201–1,245.

[5] Tse, H. H., & Troth, A. C., "Perceptions and Emotional Experiences in Differential Supervisor-Subordinate Relationships," *Leadership & Organization Development Journal* 34, no. 3 (2013): 271–283, https://doi.org/10.1108/01437731311326693.

[6] Dienesch, R., & Liden, R., "Leader-Member Exchange Model of Leadership: A Critique and Further Development," *The Academy of Management Review* 11, no. 3 (1986): 618–634, http://www.jstor.org/stable/258314.

[7] Dienesch, R., & Liden, R., "Leader-Member Exchange Model of Leadership: A Critique and Further Development," *The Academy of Management Review* 11, no. 3 (1986): 618–634, http://www.jstor.org/stable/258314.

[8] Maslyn, J. M., & Uhl-Bien, M., "Leader-Member Exchange and its Dimensions: Effects of Self-Effort and Other's Effort on Relationship Quality," *Journal of Applied Psychology* 86, no. 4 (2001): 697–708, https://doi.org/10.1037/0021-9010.86.4.697.

[9] Duchon, D., Green, S. G., & Taber, T. D., "Vertical Dyad Linkage: A Longitudinal Assessment of Antecedents, Measures, and Consequences," *Journal of Applied Psychology* 71, no. 1 (1986): 56–60, https://doi.org/10.1037/0021-9010.71.1.56.

[10] Engle, E. M., & Lord, R. G., "Implicit Theories, Self-Schemas, and Leader-Member Exchange," *Academy of Management Journal* 40, no. 4 (1997): 988–1,010, https://doi.org/10.2307/256956.

[11] Omilion-Hodges, L. M., & Baker, C. R., "Contextualizing LMX Within the Workgroup: The Effects of LMX and Justice on Relationship Quality and Resource Sharing Among Peers," *The Leadership Quarterly* 24, no. 6 (2013): 935–951, https://doi.org/10.1016/j.leaqua.2013.10.004.

[12] Chassie, M. (1984), *Vertical Dyadic Linkage Formation: Predictors and Processes Determining Quality Superior-Subordinate Relationships (Nursing, Southwest, Women),* [Doctoral dissertation, The University of Texas at Dallas], Dissertation Abstracts International Section A: Humanities and Social Sciences.

[13] Graen, G., & Uhl-Bien, M., "Relationship-Based Approach to Leadership: Development of Leader-Member Exchange (LMX) Theory of Leadership Over 25 Years: Applying a Multi-Level Multi-Domain Perspective," *The Leadership Quarterly* 6, no. 2 (1995): 219–247. https://doi.org/10.1016/1048-9843(95)90036 -5.

[14] Kim, K. I., & Organ, D. W., "Determinants of Leader-Subordinate Exchange Relationships," *Group & Organization Studies* 7, no. 1 (1982): 77–89, https://doi.org/10.1177/105960118200700107.

[15] Tse, H. H., & Troth, A. C., "Perceptions and Emotional Experiences in Differential Supervisor-Subordinate Relationships*," Leadership & Organization Development Journal* 34, no. 3 (2013): 271–283, https://doi.org/10.1108 /01437731311326693.

[16] Graen, G., & Uhl-Bien, M., "Relationship-Based Approach to Leadership: Development of Leader-Member Exchange (LMX) Theory of Leadership Over 25 Years: Applying a Multi-Level Multi-Domain Perspective," *The Leadership Quarterly* 6, no. *2* (1995): 219–247, https://doi.org/10.1016/1048-9843(95)90036 -5.

[17] Graen, G., & Uhl-Bien, M., "Relationship-Based Approach to Leadership: Development of Leader-Member Exchange (LMX) Theory of Leadership Over 25 Years: Applying a Multi-Level Multi-Domain Perspective," *The Leadership Quarterly* 6, no. *2* (1995): 219–247, https://doi.org/10.1016/1048-9843(95)90036 -5.

[18] Darrat, M., Atinc, G., & Babin, B. J., "On the Dysfunctional Consequences of Salesperson Exhaustion," *Journal of Marketing*

Theory and Practice 24, no. 2 (2016): 236–245, https://doi.org
/10.1080/10696679.2016.1130563.

[19] Graen, G., Liden, R., & Hoel, W., "Role of Leadership in the
Employee Withdrawal Process," *Journal of Applied Psychology* 67,
no. 6 (1982a): 868.

[20] Graen, G., Novak, M. A., & Sommerkamp, P., "The Effects of
Leader-Member Exchange and Job Design on Productivity and
Satisfaction: Testing a Dual Attachment Model," *Organizational
Behavior and Human Performance* 30, no. 1 (1982b): 109–131,
https://doi.org/10.1016/0030-5073(82)90236-7.

[21] Dulebohn, J. H., Bommer, W. H., Liden, R. C., Brouer, R.
L., & Ferris, G. R., "A Meta-Analysis of Antecedents and
Consequences of Leader-Member Exchange," *Journal of
Management* 38, no. 6 (2011): 1715–1759, https://doi.org/10
.1177/0149206311415280.

[22] Gerstner, C., & Day, D., "Meta-Analytic Review of Leader-
Member Exchange Theory: Correlates and Construct Issues,"
Journal of Applied Psychology, 82, no. 6 (1997): 827–844.

[23] Chen, Z., Lam, W., & Zhong, J., "Leader-Member Exchange and
Member Performance: A New Look at Individual-Level Negative
Feedback-Seeking Behavior and Team-Level Empowerment
Climate," *Journal of Applied Psychology*, 92, no. 1 (2007):
202–212, https://doi.org/10.1037/0021-9010.92.1.202.

[24] Els, C., Viljoen, J., Beer, L., & Brand-Labuschagne, L., "The
Mediating Effect of Leader-Member Exchange Between
Strengths Use and Work Engagement," *Journal of Psychology
in Africa* 26, no. 1 (2016): 22–28, https://doi.org/10.1080
/14330237.2016.1149278.

[25] Graen, G., & Uhl-Bien, M., "Relationship-Based Approach to
Leadership: Development of Leader-Member Exchange (LMX)
Theory of Leadership Over 25 Years: Applying a Multi-Level

Multi-Domain Perspective," *Quarterly* 6, no. 2 (1995): 219–247, https://doi.org/10.1016/1048-9843(95)90036-5.

26 Graen, G., "Role-Making Processes of Leadership Development," in M. D. Dunnette (ed.) *Handbook of Industrial and Organizational Psychology (*Chicago: Rand McNally, 1976): 1,201–1,245.

27 Harris, K. J., Wheeler, A. R., & Kacmar, K., "Leader-Member Exchange and Empowerment: Direct and Interactive Effects on Job Satisfaction, Turnover Intentions, and Performance*," The Leadership Quarterly* 20, no. 3 (2009): 371–382, https://doi.org /10.1016/j.leaqua.2009.03.006.

28 Duchon, D., Green, S. G., & Taber, T. D., "Vertical Dyad Linkage: A Longitudinal Assessment of Antecedents, Measures, and Consequences," *Journal of Applied Psychology* 71, no. 1 (1986)*:* 56–60, https://doi.org/10.1037/0021-9010.71.1.56.

29 Le Blanc, P. M., & González-Romá, V., "A Team-Level Investigation of the Relationship Between Leader-Member Exchange (LMX) Differentiation, and Commitment and Performance," *The Leadership Quarterly* 23, no. 3 (2012): 534–544, https://doi.org/10.1016/j.leaqua.2011.12.006.

30 Scandura, T. A., & Graen, G. B., "Moderating Effects of Initial Leader-Member Exchange Status on the Effects of a Leadership Intervention," *Journal of Applied Psychology* 69, no. 3 (1984): 428–436, https://doi.org/10.1037/0021-9010.69.3.428.

31 Fisk, G. M., & Friesen, J. P., "Perceptions of Leader Emotion Regulation and LMX as Predictors of Followers' Job Satisfaction and Organizational Citizenship Behaviors," *The Leadership Quarterly* 23, no. 1 (2012): 1–12, https://doi.org/10.1016 /j.leaqua.2011.11.001.

32 Graen, G., & Uhl-Bien, M., "Relationship-Based Approach to Leadership: Development of Leader-Member Exchange (LMX) Theory of Leadership Over 25 Years: Applying a Multi-Level

Multi-Domain Perspective," *The Leadership Quarterly* 6, no. 2 (1995): 219–247, https://doi.org/10.1016/1048-9843(95)90036 -5.

[33] Uhl-Bien, M., & Graen, G., "Self-Management and Team-Making in Cross-Functional Work Teams: Discovering the Keys to Becoming an Integrated Team," *The Journal of High Technology Management Research* 3, no. 2 (1992): 225–241.

[34] Graen, G., & Uhl-Bien, M., "Relationship-Based Approach to Leadership: Development of Leader-Member Exchange (LMX) Theory of Leadership Over 25 Years: Applying a Multi-Level Multi-Domain Perspective," *The Leadership Quarterly* 6, no. 2 (1995): 219–247, https://doi.org/10.1016/1048-9843(95)90036 -5.

[35] Nahrgang, J. D., Morgeson, F. P., & Ilies, R., "The Development of Leader-Member Exchanges: Exploring How Personality and Performance Influence Leader and Member Relationships Over Time," *Organizational Behavior and Human Decision Processes* 108, no. 2 (2009): 256–266, https://doi.org/10.1016/j.obhdp .2008.09.002.

[36] Graen, G., & Uhl-Bien, M., "Relationship-Based Approach to Leadership: Development of Leader-Member Exchange (LMX) Theory of Leadership Over 25 Years: Applying a Multi-Level Multi-Domain Perspective," *The Leadership Quarterly* 6, no. 2 (1995): 219–247, https://doi.org/10.1016/1048-9843(95)90036 -5.

[37] Tse, H., & Dasborough, M., "A Study of Emotion and Exchange in Team Member Relationships," *Group and Organization Management* 33, no. 2 (2008): 194–215.

Chapter 8: Strategies to Improve Feelings of Leader Support

[1] Pelenk, S.E., "The Medication Effect of Leader Support in the Effect of Organizational Commitment on Job Satisfaction: A Research in the Turkish Textile Business," *International Journal*

of Organizational Leadership 9 (2020): 227–242, https://doi.10
.3384/ijol.2020.60508.

[2] Pelenk, S.E., "The Medication Effect of Leader Support in the
Effect of Organizational Commitment on Job Satisfaction: A
Research in the Turkish Textile Business," *International Journal
of Organizational Leadership* 9 (2020): 227–242, https://doi.10
.3384/ijol.2020.60508.

[3] Stajkovic, A., & Lutchans, F., "Differential Effects of Incentive
Motivators on Work Performance," *Academy of Management
Journal* 44, no. 3 (2001): 580–590, https://doi.10.5465
/3069372.

[4] Lane, A., "11 Ways Highly Successful Leaders Support Their Team,"
Redbooth Business, 2021, https://redbooth.com/hub/successful-
leaders-support-their-team/.

[5] Lane, A., "11 Ways Highly Successful Leaders Support Their Team,"
Redbooth Business, 2021, https://redbooth.com/hub/successful-
leaders-support-their-team/.

[6] Li, S., Jia, R., Seufert, J., Wang, X., & Luo, J., "Ambidextrous
Leadership and Radical Innovative Capability: The Moderating
Role of Leader Support," *Creativity and Innovation Management*
29, no. 4 (2020): 621–633, https://doi.10.1111/caim.12402.

[7] Pelenk, S.E., "The Medication Effect of Leader Support in the
Effect of Organizational Commitment on Job Satisfaction: A
Research in the Turkish Textile Business," *International Journal
of Organizational Leadership* 9 (2020): 227–242, https://doi.10
.3384/ijol.2020.60508.

[8] Fritzsche, B., & Parrish, T. "Theories and Research on Job
Satisfaction," *Career Development and Counseling: Putting Theory
and Research to Work*, (2005): 180–202.

Chapter 9: Strategies to Improve Leader Trust

[1] Soderberg, A., & Romney, A., "Building Trust: How Leaders can Engender Feelings of Trust Among Followers," *Business Horizons* 65, no. 2 (2022): 173–182, https://doi.org/10.1016/j.bushor .2021.02.031.

[2] Turaga, R., "Building Trust in Teams: A Leader's Role," *The IUP Journal of Soft Skills* 7, no. 2 (2013): 13–31.

[3] Soderberg, A., & Romney, A., "Building Trust: How Leaders can Engender Feelings of Trust Among Followers," *Business Horizons* 65, no. 2 (2022): 173–182, https://doi.org/10.1016/j.bushor .2021.02.031.

[4] Soderberg, A., & Romney, A., "Building Trust: How Leaders can Engender Feelings of Trust Among Followers," *Business Horizons* 65, no. 2 (2022): 173–182, https://doi.org/10.1016/j.bushor .2021.02.031.

[5] Soderberg, A., & Romney, A., "Building Trust: How Leaders can Engender Feelings of Trust Among Followers," *Business Horizons* 65, no. 2 (2022): 173–182, https://doi.org/10.1016/j.bushor .2021.02.031.

[6] Soderberg, A., & Romney, A., "Building Trust: How Leaders can Engender Feelings of Trust Among Followers," *Business Horizons* 65, no. 2 (2022): 173–182, https://doi.org/10.1016/j.bushor .2021.02.031.

[7] Newbold, K., "Top 5 Ways to Treat Gossip in Your Practice," Veterinary Team Brief (2014): 12–13.

[8] Soderberg, A., & Romney, A., "Building Trust: How Leaders can Engender Feelings of Trust Among Followers," *Business Horizons* 65, no. 2 (2022): 173–182, https://doi.org/10.1016/j.bushor .2021.02.031.

[9] Newbold, K., "Top 5 Ways to Treat Gossip in Your Practice," Veterinary Team Brief (2014): 12–13.

[10] Newbold, K., "Top 5 Ways to Treat Gossip in Your Practice," Veterinary Team Brief (2014): 12–13.

Chapter 10: Strategies to Improve Leader Communication

[1] Soderberg, A., & Romney, A., "Building Trust: How Leaders can Engender Feelings of Trust Among Followers," *Business Horizons* 65, no. 2 (2022): 173–182.

[2] Gibson, C. & Manuel, J., "Building Trust," *Virtual Teams that Work,* (San Francisco: Jossey Bass, 2003), 59–86.

[3] Kanter, R., "Collaborative Advantage: The Art of Alliances," *Harvard Business Review* 72, no. 4 (1994): 96–108.

[4] Anders, R., "Practical Tips for Effective Communication," *Nursing Management* 52, no. 6 (2021): 10–13.

[5] Anders, R., "Practical Tips for Effective Communication," *Nursing Management* 52, no. 6 (2021): 10–13.

[6] Soderberg, A., & Romney, A., "Building Trust: How Leaders can Engender Feelings of Trust Among Followers," *Business Horizons* 65, no. 2 (2022): 173–182.

[7] Soderberg, A., & Romney, A., "Building Trust: How Leaders can Engender Feelings of Trust Among Followers," *Business Horizons,* 65, no. 2 (2022): 173–182.

[8] Anders, R., "Practical Tips for Effective Communication," *Nursing Management* 52, no. 6 (2021): 10–13.

[9] Henderson, A., "Leadership and Communication: What are the Imperatives?" *Journal of Nursing Management* 23 (2015): 693–694, https://doi.10.1111/jonm.12336.

[10] Soderberg, A., & Romney, A., "Building Trust: How Leaders can Engender Feelings of Trust Among Followers," *Business Horizons* 65, no. 2 (2022): 173–182.

[11] Henderson, A., "Leadership and Communication: What are the Imperatives?" *Journal of Nursing Management* 23 (2015): 693–694, https://doi.10.1111/jonm.12336.

[12] Anders, R., "Practical Tips for Effective Communication," *Nursing Management* 52, no. 6 (2021): 10–13.

[13] Anders, R., "Practical Tips for Effective Communication," *Nursing Management* 52, no. 6 (2021): 10–13.

Chapter 11: Strategies to Improve Leader & Employee Relationships

[1] Graen, G., & Uhl-Bien, M., "Relationship-Based Approach to Leadership: Development of Leader-Member Exchange (LMX) Theory of Leadership Over 25 Years: Applying a Multi-Level Multi-Domain Perspective," *The Leadership Quarterly* 6, no. 2 (1995): 219–247, https://doi.org/10.1016/1048-9843(95)90036-5.

[2] Sims, H, & Manz, C., "Observing Leader Behavior: Toward Reciprocal Determinism in Leadership Theory," *Journal of Applied Psychology* 69, no. 2 (1984): 222–232, https://doi.org/10.1037/0021-9010.69.2.222.

[3] Graen, G., & Uhl-Bien, M., "The Transformation of Professionals into Self-Managing and Partially Self-Designing Contributions," *Journal of Management Systems* 3, no. 3 (1991): 25–39.

[4] Graen G., & Scandura, T., "Toward a Psychology of Dyadic Organizing," *Research in Organizational Behavior* 9 (1987): 175–208.

[5] Graen, G., & Uhl-Bien, M., "The Transformation of Professionals into Self-Managing and Partially Self-Designing Contributions," *Journal of Management Systems* 3, no. 3 (1991): 25–39.

[6] Graen, G., & Uhl-Bien, M., "Relationship-Based Approach to Leadership: Development of Leader-Member Exchange (LMX) Theory of Leadership Over 25 Years: Applying a Multi-Level

Multi-Domain Perspective," *The Leadership Quarterly* 6, no. 2 (1995): 219–247, https://doi.org/10.1016/1048-9843(95)90036 -5.

7 Dienesch, R., & Liden, R., "Leader-Member Exchange Model of Leadership: A Critique and Further Development," *The Academy of Management Review* 11, no. 3 (1986): 618–634, https://www .jstor.org/stable/258314.

8 Engle, E., & Lord, R., "Implicit Theories, Self-Schemas, and Leader-Member Exchange," *Academy of Management Journal* 40, no. 4 (1997): 988–1,010, https://doi.org/10.2307/256956.

9 Graen, G., & Uhl-Bien, M., "Relationship-Based Approach to Leadership: Development of Leader-Member Exchange (LMX) Theory of Leadership Over 25 Years: Applying a Multi-Level Multi-Domain Perspective," *The Leadership Quarterly* 6, no. *2* (1995): 219–247, https://doi.org/10.1016/1048-9843(95)90036 -5.

10 Graen, G., & Uhl-Bien, M., "The Transformation of Professionals into Self-Managing and Partially Self-Designing Contributions," *Journal of Management Systems* 3, no. 3 (1991): 25–39.

11 Gerstner, C., & Day, D., "Meta-Analytic Review of Leader-Member Exchange Theory: Correlates and Construct Issues," *Journal of Applied Psychology* 82, no.6 (1997): 827–844.

Chapter 12: Organizational Implications of Improved Leader Support

1 Graen, G., & Uhl-Bien, M., "Relationship-Based Approach to Leadership: Development of Leader-Member Exchange (LMX) Theory of Leadership Over 25 Years: Applying a Multi-Level Multi-Domain Perspective," *The Leadership Quarterly* 6, no. 2 (1995): 219–247, https://doi.org/10.1016/1048-9843(95)90036 -5.

2 Manuti, A., Presti, A., & Giancaspro, M., "The Association of HRM Practices with Organizational Citizenship Behaviors: The

Mediating Role of Work Engagement, Perceived Organizational Support and Leader-Member Exchange," *BPA–Applied Psychology Bulletin* 292 (2021).

[3] Gerstner, D., & Day, D., "Meta-Analytic Review of Leader-Member Exchange Theory: Correlates and Construct Issues," *Journal of Applied Psychology* 82, no. 6 (1997): 827–844.

[4] Nahrgang, J., Morgeson, F., & Ilies, R., "The Development of Leader-Member Exchanges: Exploring How Personality and Performance Influence Leader and Member Relationships Over Time," *Organizational Behavior and Human Decision Processes* 108, no. 2 (2009): 256–266, https://doi.org/10.1016/j.obhdp.2008.09.002.

[5] Graen, G., & Uhl-Bien, M., "Relationship-Based Approach to Leadership: Development of Leader-Member Exchange (LMX) Theory of Leadership Over 25 Years: Applying a Multi-Level Multi-Domain Perspective," *The Leadership Quarterly* 6, no. 2 (1995): 219–247, https://doi.org/10.1016/1048-9843(95)90036-5.

[6] Graen, G., & Uhl-Bien, M., "Relationship-Based Approach to Leadership: Development of Leader-Member Exchange (LMX) Theory of Leadership Over 25 Years: Applying a Multi-Level Multi-Domain Perspective," *The Leadership Quarterly* 6, no. 2 (1995): 219–247, https://doi.org/10.1016/1048-9843(95)90036-5.

[7] Darret, M., Atinc, G., & Babib, B., "On the Dysfunctional Consequences of Salesperson Exhaustion," *Journal of Marketing Theory and Practice* 24, no. 2 (2016): 236–245, https://doi.org/10.1080/10696679.2016.1130563.

[8] Harris, K., Wheeler, A., & Kacmar, K., "Leader-Member Exchange and Empowerment: Direct and Interactive Effects on Job Satisfaction, Turnover Intentions, and Performance," *The Leadership Quarterly* 20, no. 3 (2009): 371–382, https://doi.org/10.1016/j.leaqua.2009.03.006.

[9] Ahmed, I., Ismail, W., Amin, S., & Ramzan, M., "Influence of Relationship of POS, LMX and Organizational Commitment on Turnover Intentions," *Organization Development Journal* 31, no. 1 (2013): 55–68.

Julie Kovencz

has been a healthcare human resources professional for the last 14 years. She achieved her Doctorate in Strategic Leadership from Southeastern University, her Master's in Human Resource Development from Clemson University, her PHR certification from HRIC, and her SHRM-CP certification from SHRM. Julie lives in Florida with her son, Cody, along with their dog and two cats.

Connect with the Author

LinkedIn:
https://www.linkedin.com/in/julie-kovencz-mhrd-phr/

Email:
kovenczj@hotmail.com

Leave a Review

If you enjoyed reading *Retaining Your Healthcare Heroes*, please consider leaving a review on the platform of your choice. Reviews help self-published authors find more readers like yourself.

www.ingramcontent.com/pod-product-compliance
Lightning Source LLC
Chambersburg PA
CBHW060235030426
42335CB00014B/1462